DAVID FEHERTY

Go F+F!

Feherty

Go For It!

DAVID FEHERTY

BLACK IRISH ENTERTAINMENT LLC

LOS ANGELES   NEW YORK

BLACK IRISH ENTERTAINMENT LLC 65
CENTRAL PARK WEST
NEW YORK, NY 10023

COPYRIGHT © 2002 BY DAVID FEHERTY
BOOK DESIGN BY HSC AND ASSOCIATES
BACK COVER ARTWORK AND
INTERIOR ILLUSTRATIONS BY VICTOR JUHASZ

FIRST BLACK IRISH ENTERTAINMENT EDITION JUNE 2013

FOR INFORMATION ABOUT SPECIAL DISCOUNTS FOR BULK PURCHASES
PLEASE VISIT WWW.BLACKIRISHBOOKS.COM

TRADE PAPERBACK ISBN: 978-1936891061

EBOOK ISBN: 978-1936891153

For Ken Still, a decent, honest man (unlike me).

Table of Contents

Foreword

I know what you're thinking. Here's Feherty again with more mindless ramblings through the tangled Y-fronts of his warped mind. And as usual, this book is a rather large bucket filled to the brim with irrelevant drivel about everything but what you really want to read about, golf. Wrapped up in four blankets of inanity, one dust jacket per season with yours truly looking as if I'd just been released from shock therapy, this tome has been bought either by you, or for you by someone even stupider than you.

But I like people like that – in fact, I'm friends with most of my really good friends *simply because* they're idiots. When you think about it, the stupid things people do, and the stupid ways in which they act, are usually the very things that endear them to us in the first place. They make us feel clever, so we love them, and then we do something equally stupid and they love us back, and the world turns. Take a look anywhere in the world where there is trouble and I guarantee you'll find a bunch of idiots who actually believe that they're the only ones who are right. Which is hysterical, because any idiot can see that they're wrong. Possibly.

Anyway, if you are one of the idiots who read my column, you may be in this book, for after each excerpt shamelessly plundered from *Golf Magazine*, there is a reader's letter, followed by my response. All of these epistles are from loyal disciples too, because I'm far too clever to get any negative mail.

In puris naturalibus!

David Feherty

Winter

Fear of Flying

It's early in the season, but already I'm tired of flying.

I never get tired of being there, mind you. But these days it's getting there that's the problem. For a start, I have a bad relationship with electric appliances, so anything that involves computers (like e-tickets) has a high disaster potential.

My toaster's tried to kill me twice, my cell phone treats me like I've stolen it, and I've completely lost it with those GPS systems in some vehicles. I don't mind a machine that thinks it's smarter than me as long as it keeps its opinion to itself, but when one starts giving orders, I have to answer back.

"Make your next legal U-turn," it keeps telling me, and I'm not having it. I'll be happy when I've made one of the damn things carsick enough for it to want to get out of the vehicle by itself.

And all this electronic scanning stuff, beeping wands, and pinging portals—I have a bad time with them, too. I could pay for stuff twice at a department store and tape both receipts to my forehead, but I still set off the alarm and get the full Winona from some bald guy in a suit and sunglasses.

It's even worse at the airport. It's like watching Goldmember trying to get through security. I've spent more time in the crucified position than one of Michelangelo's models, and there is one employee at DFW International Airport who could make a clay model of my buttocks with his eyes closed.

Maybe it's the unavoidable air of total dried-up-and-pissed-off-ness I exude when I travel that gives security personnel the impression I need to be detained and invaded. I've tried being cheerful and silly, but they see right through it, and it's Gropesville-here-I-come.

Once, I was trying to get out of Jackson, Mississippi. Earlier, I had checked a couple of shotguns at the American Airlines counter, an interesting experience to say the least. It's harder to get a damned corkscrew on an airplane these days.

My shotguns were broken down and packed in a hard case, unloaded as per regulation, but it was with some surprise that I watched the nice lady fit one of those wee swabby things into her stick-whatsit, and start to rub it all over the barrels, bolts, receivers, etc.

I'd been missing sporting clays for two days, and hadn't had time to clean the equipment, so her cloth was picking up powder, grease, and uh, well, it seemed weird that she was doing it, that's all.

So I asked her. "Excuse me ma'am, but isn't that machine supposed to detect explosives?" She looked pityingly at me over the top of her glasses and said, "Uh-huh, honey, that's just exactly what it does," like she was explaining to Martha Burk why the Masters couldn't be moved to Royal St. George's.

OK, then, this ought to be interesting, I thought, waiting for the alarm and bracing myself for the inevitable rough rubber-gloving from a large man with a trapdoor in the seat of his confederate-flag underpants. She-Who-Must-Be-Obeyed's family is from Mississippi, so I know the story. These people think *Deliverance* is a love story. Into the Swabnosticator went the oily rag, and "bing" went the frigging green light! What a bummer, I could have brought the C4 and the rocket launcher after all.

The loneliest place in the world might be the American Airlines departure gates in this place on a Sunday afternoon. I finish my book, and figure I'll be able to pick up another before I get on the plane to Dallas, but no dice. I have Norah Jones in my CD player, which croaks halfway through the first track. There's no way to get a couple of AA batteries, and adding insult is Christina Aguilera on the only television in the terminal. She's just one of the ghastly bottle-blond 20-something warblers I can't stand.

Evidently, the national anthem isn't about the nation anymore, but about how much of Miss Aguilera's backside she can reveal. To defend the flag this little trollop is wearing, and the freedom for which it stands, we send our young men and women into harm's way. Play it like this for an old Marine and he'd put his hand over his eyes, not his heart. And Norah Jones, who licks my ears with plain, sweet inflection against a velvet backdrop of her own divine accompaniment, while actually sitting still (what a concept), lies dead in my backpack. How can this get worse?

An hour later, I'm sitting on the plane, staring dully at the now obsolete telephone in the back of the seat in front of me, wondering why they can't replace them with a fuselage-safe gun that can only be released by a switch in the cockpit. That way, the next time some idiot stands up with a box cutter, a passenger could welcome him to America by shooting his stupid ass, with the help of the captain. Just a thought.

Meanwhile I'm trying not to listen to half of an obnoxiously loud cell phone conversation involving the orange-tan-in-a-bottle cretin in the next seat. I make ugly eye contact, and he winks at me! This trip is turning into a living hell. His bulging man-breasts are quivering through some kind of shimmering, black Lycra shirt as he removes a patent leather Gucci loafer to pick something ghastly off his fungus-encrusted big toe. Lovely. As it turns out, he's leaving a message, and there is a communal nod of satisfaction around the cabin when he starts with, "Hey Lenny, this is Dick."

Gloria the flight attendant asks me if I want the gray meat or the orange pasta. I can't make up my mind, so I opt for the colorless Absolut instead. Then Gucci Dick interrupts his all-important message to point a chubby finger and thumb pretend-gun at Gloria, makes a double clicking sound with his chewing gum, winks again, and says he'll have my pasta along with his steak—"Capisce, toots?" Toots shoots him a look that would stop a clock, but Dick is unfazed, and damnit, I feel like an extra in "The Sopranos."

Out of options for a diversion, I realize I'm going to have to delve between the sheets of the last literary option for the professional traveler, and the single clearest indicator of my abject surrender to crushing boredom: SkyMall. Through sheer force of habit, I start at the back. Oh good, it's an advertisement for a medical jet service that will, should Gucci Dick suffer a massive coronary in Venezuela, whisk him back to Miami to be miraculously resuscitated by a Venezuelan doctor.

A page forward, we have the "Earl of Houghton Elephant" wall mount, which weighs in at a suspiciously cheesy eight pounds. I can hardly contain myself when I find that for a mere $295, I can be the proud owner of "Glamdring," the sword of Gandalf. Even better, while I'm visiting Middle-Earth, for less than half of that I can thrust my middle finger into "Galadriel's Ring" and in that time-honored Upper-Earth tradition, indicate to the nearest Orc that his presence is not necessary. Splendid! This flight is fairly winging by now.

In the "Inspiring Artwork" section, for $139.99, I can get a wood-framed photo of a big-ass rock with a scrawny tree growing out of it, with the gooseflesh-raising statement printed underneath: "Unless you try to do something beyond what you have already mastered, you will never grow."

Brilliant, although even if the English language is beyond what you have already mastered, you might get a job writing crappy copy for inspiring art.

The best photo in here is of Tony Little, pony-tailed and splay-legged in spandex with a dung-eating grin that I swear makes him look almost more punchable than Dr. Phil. Tony is on his Gazelle Freestyle, a total aerobic workout. Anyone who buys one of those things needs a good thrashing.

The pet section is for the spectacularly short of sense. One product that caught my attention was the weatherproof dog bed, which I might actually buy if I ever get a weatherproof dog. Like Willard the Wonder Mutt would ever sleep outside. Hah!

An attempt to deliver such an item to our house would be a bad idea, for if the neighborhood dog known as "Death to Squirrels" ever got wind of it, the mailman would be performing the task with 20 pounds of growling terrier dangling from either cheek.

The stupefying power of SkyMall is not to be underestimated. If not for our descent into Dallas, I might have been tempted into ordering a roll of talking toilet paper. Gucci Dick had nodded off a while ago, wearing the grim expression of a man who knew he was being written about but couldn't protest because it would be a damning admission that he was a peeping Tom. So he decided to be a sleeping Dick instead.

Time to turn off approved electronic devices. This trip was a bummer all right, and if you're on one, I hope you have more to read than this.

Could you give us readers an idea of what a week is like as a commentator? Do you get to play the course before you commentate on it? Thanks.

— *Jeffrey Formanczyk, East Lansing, Michigan*

MONDAY: Hopefully got in Sunday night if there wasn't a goddamn playoff and I missed the flight home again. Sleep late. Have She-Who-Must-Be-Obeyed bring in two lightly boiled with crisp bacon, golden toasted scones with clotted cream, raspberry jam, and piping hot café au lait right to the bedroom. Nap. Stumble out of bed around 2:30. Slip on smoking jacket and ascot, call McCord to hear report of how magnificent I was yesterday. After flicking their turds off my lawn and onto the neighbor's, take Sigmoid and Willard for walkies. Snifter or two of Ketel One and grapefruit. Dinner. Weak attempt at sex (with myself). Take two Ambien and collapse, hopefully in bed.

TUESDAY: Car pool duty. Try to remain in check while picking up other rich people's offspring. Meet with Rory's teacher. Try to convince her he was only kidding about shooting up the gym class. Double the dose on the Ritalin. Lunch with financial planner. Call agent and demand more bookings, need more money. Drive to shotgun club. Shoot 400 rounds of 28 gauge, miss 30 percent. Nap. Dinner. Field-test new case of Napa Valley Silver Oak Cab.

WEDNESDAY: Same as Tuesday, unless I'm doing cable. Then I leave for tournament.

THURSDAY: Same as Wednesday unless I'm on cable, then I eat breakfast in hotel, go to course, eat lunch in CBS compound. Nap. Go to booth and perform extensive preparation for broadcast, which consists of: sound check and nap. Go back to hotel, go to bar and run up huge tab. Go to dinner with producer Lance and Barrow and Kostis. Let Kostis pick wine if Lance is buying.

FRIDAY: Same as Thursday.

SATURDAY AND SUNDAY: After I get to CBS compound, get trussed up in diabolical RF harness and hang antennas off dubious appendages. Walk all 18 with leaders while making brilliant commentary and reading greens as if I played on them all my life. Sweating like a lifer meeting the parole board for his last shot at getting out. Gold Bond powder shooting out my nose. Bar. Dinner, if I am ambulatory.

Rubberize My Room

Well, here we are in that great normality rehab of the West—Los Angeles. It's the Nissan Open at lovely Riviera Country Club, just off the Sunset Strip, between Beverly Hills and Malibu, teetering on the crusty spine of the San Andreas fault. This place always reminds me of an old Warren Zevon song: *"And if California slides into the ocean / as the mystics and statistics say it will / I believe this motel will be standing / until I pay my bill."*

I love a mentally unbalanced pessimist. There are more raving nutcases per square mile in this state than in any other. I'm convinced of it, and what's more, they're all in contact with one another. They have little earpieces hanging down to their concealed cell phones, and they walk around talking, either to themselves or each other, I'm not sure which. Wearing anything but black appears to be totally illegal, and thin-soled shoes are way out. Our hotel is a perfect example. We've stayed here for years, and it used to be the Westwood Marquis, until last year when we checked in, and it had been transformed into "The W Los Angeles."

The old Marquis was nasty, and had a bar like a funeral home, all purple velvet and chintz, with stuffed old people and waiters that hadn't seen daylight in years. Now, the "W" is the exact opposite. It's gone from a funeral home, to a cross between a haunted house, a mental hospital, and a scene from the "The Matrix." All the staff wear black, have black headsets, black tattoos, pierced whatsits, and robotic grins. Even the elevators have black and purple lights. They had a rolling blackout here last week, and no one in this hotel noticed.

To gain entrance to the hotel, you now have to navigate a set of glass steps, under which a waterfall cascades to the sidewalk. I think it must be a nightmare when the salmon are mating. The bar has been transformed into a techno-throbbing oystercluster, and is now filled with the most confusing array of furniture I have ever seen. It is completely impossible to tell whether you should be sitting on it, or eating off it, so everyone just stands around looking cool, wishing they could smoke, which is also illegal, unless you happen to be under a fire blanket in neighboring Nevada.

This is the end of the West Coast Swing for us at CBS, and the perfect hotel to cap it off. The whole crew is on the edge of madness anyway. Well, except for McCord, who fell over that one year ago. Strangely enough, he's the only one who looks halfway comfortable in the bar. I think it's the shoes.

It's also Grammy week here in L.A., so the place is particularly full of people who spend far too much time in front of the mirror. I'm hiding in my room for the rest of the week. Everything I need is here: The History Channel, long neck Budweisers, a 425 thread count on the bed, and a sign that says "Leave me alone" hanging on the doorknob. Bring on the Masters.

Hi David. About two years ago you actually phoned me to answer a question I had asked. I ended up sending you a green Canadian Coast Guard shirt. Just a couple of weeks ago you MC'd Mike Weir's charity tournament in Sarnia. I was standing right beside you but didn't have the balls to say "hi" because I was helping a journalist friend of mine and didn't think it would be professional. Anyway, next time you're in Sarnia I'd like to smoke a nicely aged Cuban and perhaps have a little nip at the course with you. I'll be the press guy watching the pro's golf swing instead of taking shots! Hope to see you next year.

— *Steve Klamer*

Weir's gig is one of my favorites. No one considers it professional to say hello to me. I prefer amateurs anyway; they're less pretentious. And just for the record, I don't think you should be smoking "nicely aged Cubans," my friend. I mean, how would you like it if Castro fired up one of our senior citizens? And if we're gonna have a nip or two, let's do it in a nice pub. The only time I set foot on an actual course these days is when CBS is paying me.

Method to the Madness

A little while ago, it occurred to me that I'd been with CBS Sports for almost six years and I still had no idea how the hell we ever get a show on the air without loss of life, or at the very least, someone having a good cry. On the screen, golf is so demure and tranquil that for the average viewer it's impossible to imagine the utter chaos that frequently occurs behind the scenes.

It's kind of like the difference in atmosphere between the dining room and the kitchen of an elegant, five-star restaurant. Out front, the dapper maitre d' might be popping the cork on a nice bottle of bubbly and placing a gleaming Waterford flute on crisp, white linen. But in the back, an Immigration and Naturalization Service official has just broken up a knife fight between the club-footed Guatemalan pastry chef, who found a Lucky Strike butt in his tiramisu, and an Irish dishwasher, who is yelling down the telephone at his bookmaker and refuses to hang up. Happens all the time, I'm sure.

Our restaurant has 18 tables, waited on by seven big-mouthed, attitudinally-challenged announcers, and as many as 150 awkward diners, all of which makes the television compound the kitchen from hell. In virtually every other televised sport, there is one arena, one reasonably sized ball, and one story.

With golf, you have at any given moment several tiny

projectiles whizzing through the airspace in several different areas, with several different people yelling at them to stop, go, get up, come down, buzz off, or whatever. Someone has to decide which shot to take, which microphone to open, which graphic to insert, and which announcer should be dragged out of his tower and beaten within an inch of his life. That person is Lance Barrow, the coordinating producer of CBS golf.

An announcer has the easiest job in television, unless of course his name is Nantz, but that's a whole 'nother column. Follow the optic fiber out of the tower, through the invisible slits cut into the fairway, under the heavy rubber conduits that straddle the cart paths and service roads, into the television compound, and you'll find the multimillion-dollar, digital 18-wheeler, code-named DX6. With its thundering air-conditioning unit sucking the moisture away from miles of wiring, and darkness broken by a mere 200 flickering monitors, this is the nerve center, a place where many a nerve has been shattered.

On the front row, closest to the myriad monitors, is the A-Team. The only difference between us and the original is that we are astonished when a plan comes together. Facing golf's wailing wall, there is the athletic yet strangely chubby Jim Rikhoff, who came from a good family but somehow developed a few ways about him that just aren't right. He is Lance's left eye and ear, and occasionally does nostril duty.

Moving left to right, there's Lance—309 pounds of deep-fried, quivering manhood, shaped like some giant, ethereal, Rubenesque cherub on the domed ceiling of an ancient chapel. He wears a constant and undying expression that would suggest he just realized he was about to miss God's last slice of pizza. He's on air, on point, and carrying on board enough iced tea to float Greg Norman's new yacht.

On the course, Eldrick "Tiger" Woods is clearly the best and in the truck, Lance "Rhino" Barrow is equally dominant. To his right is director Steve Milton, legendary son of production great Chuck Milton, who has lately been trying out as a Chippendale dancer in his spare time. Steve is Lance's right eye and right ear, and in times of great tension can occasionally be heard screaming "Uncle!" from under the big man's right armpit.

On Steve's right is Norm Patterson, comatose every minute we're not on the air but with a heart rate of 311 every minute we are. Norm's job is to filter out the screaming, dodge the bitch-slapping, and switch to the correct camera at the correct time.

Behind the front row, the rest of the crew of DX6 is tucked away in some dim corner, lurking behind heavy black drapes, or locked behind soundproof doors. It's a mobile mental hospital, inhabited by an incredible bunch of brilliant freaks, none of whom could work anywhere but in television.

We have three machines that play back and record at the same time (a digital concept that reduces my IQ from one to zero every time I try to understand it). They are nicknamed Elvis, Python, and Mongoose. Recently, we lost Big Mike Hoskins, our Elvis operator, who died of a heart attack a couple of days after having his stomach stapled. Mike was big in more ways than one. He was funny, generous, kind. He will be deeply missed and fondly remembered by all who were lucky enough to work with him.

It's Lance's job to produce a show out of all this, and I

still don't know how he does it. It must be a conjuring trick. I understand the part about it being a production, but the thought of being responsible for coordinating it is simply too much for me to bear.

Way too many things can go wrong. I don't have enough space in this column, and there probably aren't enough words in the English language to describe adequately the potential for disaster during the course of even one of our shorter telecasts, say a two-hour show, but I'll toss out a few scenarios. Here goes, and for the sake of continuity, I'll start with the second.

2. Getting behind on commercials. The network sells a certain number of commercial slots each hour and if Lance doesn't get them in, let's just say he won't keep his Coordinating Producer of the Month parking space next to the catering truck.

1. Some dolt with a microphone stands on a moving cable. Enough said.

3. All of a sudden, a top player has trouble pulling the trigger. Okay, on the face of it this doesn't sound like a total disaster, but the producer of a golf telecast must have a sense of timing and know just how long it will be before a player starts his swing. At any given time, there may be half a dozen players at various stages of their pre-shot routines, and the task of covering each relevant shot without relying too heavily on tape is daunting. We can't exactly put up on the screen, "Coming up next, Between 45 and 60 Minutes."

9. Someone in the Porta Potti. Lance doesn't drink, which, given the nature of his job, is totally mind-boggling. He does consume roughly a gallon of unflavored iced tea per show. This

brings Porta Potti placement and access right onto one of the monitors. As I mentioned, Lance is a big man and when he has to get out of the truck, down the steps, into the squirtatorium, lose a four-pinter, and get back before the commercial break is over, you'd better not be in his way. Think of that giant, rolling rock in *"Raiders of the Lost Ark"* and you get the idea.

2. (Again) An announcer's microphone goes down. (Actually, now that I think of it, Lance has never considered this a problem.)

Anyway, you probably have a small idea of just how difficult it is to coordinate all the elements that go into a golf show. Timing is crucial and the pressure is enormous. Lance has always said that we're a family at CBS golf and he's dead right. We squabble, we compete, and we're weird enough, but Big Daddy always covers our backs.

He's kind of like the giant, sweaty captain of a ship designed by Heath Robinson. It's not pretty, and there's no way it should float, but no matter how rough the sea, Captain Barrow will bring her home.

You have a sick, twisted, and obviously perverted sense of humor. That must be why I think you are the funniest guy since Lewis Grizzard. If I could put together a fantasy foursome for a round of golf, you would be first on the list, right in front of Lee and Arnold. We might not do that much damage to par, but we could seriously deplete a stock of frosty cold Dos Equis dark beer and I'm sure we could sufficiently terrorize all who came in contact with us.

Thanks for the tip on the III Forks Steak House in Dallas. It is now my favorite pit stop when I come back to Texas to visit my family. I had the opportunity to meet Rick there, and I believe everything he told me about you. I don't know if you are a barbecue aficionado or not, but if so, take a drive down to Waco some weekend and try Underwoods. It's a Texas tradition that is slowly dying out. Keep it on the short grass.

— *Gerry Calk, Columbia, South Carolina*
(grew up in Coleman, Texas)

Did you invent that stuff I put around my windows every fall? You must be one wealthy son of a gun. Incidentally, I don't care where you grew up. What is it with Texans? Why they are compelled to tell everyone where they're from all the time? Who cares? By the way, I'm from here too.

Why would you put a Mexican, a Pennsylvanian, and an Irishman together? Sounds like the beginning of a really bad joke. Thanks for letting me know about talking to Rick about my recommendation. I have a commission deal with him and I think he's been slow playing me, if you get my drift. I'm going to check the register receipts against the list he sends me and I had better see your name or I'm gonna hit Rick so hard, he'll have to wash his underpants to clean his teeth. God, I'm starting to sound like a Texan. Thank God the season has started.

Everyone's an Expert

Yesterday was the last CBS golf show of our regular season, and I thought I'd caught a break when the bad weather moved in, and the PGA Tour decided they were going to go early, in order to get the round in. Nice final group too, with Furyk and Woods for me to follow. All done by 1 p.m. Eastern, a 3:30 American flight from Cleveland to Dallas, home in time for tea and crumpets. A lovely way to finish.

Yeah, right. Halfway into the playoff I was ready to do a Tonya Harding on one of the combatants, and I didn't care which. In retrospect I probably would have been better off attacking Jim Furyk because at least I could have outrun Fluff.

I ended up walking up and down that hill at 17 and 18 four-and-a-half times yesterday, and on the last occasion I got a damned good soaking for my trouble. A few hours later though, I was dry on the outside anyway, buried under the lip of the bar at Hopkins International, nursing a tumbler of lighter fluid and, stranger than fiction, watching the show on TV.

I don't remember the last time I actually saw a golf telecast of which I had been a part. Anyway, there was a gaggle of interested viewers in the front row, craning their necks upward at the action, and—horror of horrors—none of them knew who the hell I was. I waited for myself to say something and then ordered another biff, in exactly the same accent.

Nope, not a taker among the bastards.

"Damn that Tiger Woods," I thought. I surveyed the crowd, and listened to some snippets of conversation. To my left, there were a couple of Top Fuel mechanics who had blown the setup of their engine earlier that day, a software rep who was trying to pick up a lady who sold phone systems, and a male flight attendant who was trying to pick up the software rep.

To my right, a couple of sans-a-belt types, one who was wearing an NEC shirt. All of them had two things in common. They were experts on Tiger Woods, and of the opinion he would prevail over the white stiff he was playing against. The guy's swing was a joke, for a start.

I'm thinking, "This is unbelievable!" A few years ago, none of these people would have noticed the golf tournament flickering above them and now they all know who's going to win it, long before it's over.

I'm not sure which is worse, but I know one thing: Wadkins, the idiot, is supposed to be on my flight, and there's no sign of him anywhere. I hit his number on my cell phone. Turns out he's upstairs in the Admiral's club, watching it on his own, with his $500 Ferragamo loafers up on the back of the chair in front of him. I tell him to get his cashmere-clad ass down to join me in the cheap seats, because at least that way I can talk to someone who's smart enough to know I'm famous.

Nobody in this dump gives a damn about anyone but Tiger Woods. I mean, how are you supposed to act like an expert in your field if you're surrounded by dummies who know as much as you?

Enough with this golf, bring on football.

What is your best advice for the new-to-the-game player?

—*Jeff Tessing, Deptford, New Jersey*

The next time you're in London, stop in at the Holland and Holland store in the Mayfair section of the city. Go straight to the counter and ask for Cavendish. Just as there will always be an England, there will always be a chap named Cavendish at Holland and Holland. Tell him you want an over/under with upgraded French black walnut burled wood and gold engraved side locks with a hunting scene. He will present you with a bill for about $55,000. Pay it without question. When you get the gun home, find a really ratty gun club. You know, the ones with the toothless, tattooed woman behind the counter who during breaks goes out and picks up the unbroken targets in the field? Then never go near a golf course again and we'll all be the better for it.

Urinanalyst

Well, the Gold Bond Medicated Powder season is open, the first event having been the Byron Nelson. I carry a bottle of it in my hip pocket, and last week I made a fortune selling it by the gram to the players and caddies. David Duval doesn't sweat at all, and I think he's an alien. His pulse rate at rest is about 38. That's Tour de France stuff right there.

Robert Damron (Damright) was the main story, of course, but the thing that interested me the most about last week was the varmint problem we had at CBS. At the TPC Four Seasons Resort we have a large nutria population, which does considerable damage to the golf course by nibbling away at the roots of water plants, and burrowing under the banks of the hazards. Last week, however, they were provided with a smorgasbord of fiber optic cable, to which they unfortunately took a liking.

Now rodentia and math are two of the subjects in which I am particularly strong, but for the life of me, I do not understand why an animal that is half rat, one-third hamster, three-quarters giant gerbil, with more than a smidgeon of beaver thrown in, would find plastic and glass fiber appetizing in the slightest. I tried it myself, and it's ghastly.

But stranger than this is the method we had to employ to repel the orange-toothed little buggers: coyote pee. Yes, I said coyote pee, and personally, I thought it actually improved the taste of the cable slightly. Five cases of the stuff we bought, and I have to say, being a born-again Texan, I was a little disappointed they weren't longnecks. Apparently though, a little predator pee goes a long way in scaring off predator chow. My question is this: Who the hell collects the stuff, and how the hell do they do it? I mean, it's not just coyote we're talking about here either. You can buy bobcat whiz and bear tinkle as well! Talk about a nasty job. These creatures are pretty grumpy first thing in the morning, I'm sure. I can only imagine how hard it would be to catheterize a bobcat. "Hold still there, Fang, this might sting a little." I have this image of the guy behind the counter at the Squirtatorium, covered from head to foot in Band-Aids. The stuff has to be synthetic, surely.

The whole nutria problem is of our own making, as usual. They were introduced here from South America years ago by the fur industry, which of course has recently been skinned alive, and a good thing, too. It's a classic example of: if a thing isn't here in the first place, it's probably not needed. Although, I have to admit, I kind of fall into that category myself.

I've had an idea. I took Willard the Wonder Mutt out for his morning constitutional today, and he pitched a nine-squirter. What a waste, I thought. Here I have a natural born predator, whose sole objective in life is the complete destruction of all squirrel life on earth, and his whiz, which would have any self-respecting nutria quivering like Tim Herron on the follow-through, is being squandered on the hubcaps of my neighbors' cars. Now, I know I have a funnel and a pair of thick gloves somewhere.

I have been a big fan for years and really enjoy your columns. How long, on average, does it take you to come up with answers to these questions? Do you just rattle them off or do you need hours to make them sound funny? I know this is not golf related, but it gives you a chance to talk about yourself.

— *Geoff Povinelli, Magnolia, Texas*

Fortunately the only people who write to me are complete idiots. This makes it very simple to answer their questions. In fact, sometimes I just ignore them and write something completely irrelevant. (Rather like this.)

Hey, on the other hand, what do mean, "funny"? I'll have you know I don't think there is anything funny at all about my responses. And I don't need to spend time talking about myself. That's what I pay my friends to do. Sorry, I'm being harsh. Thanks for your support.

Ad Addict

I don't get to see commercials when I'm working on a golf telecast, but after a few months of thumbing my remote in the off-season, I feel I've gotten myself up to speed. I'm at a stage in my career (retired) when, unlike most golfers, I'm not really looking for something that's going to make me brilliant overnight. I just want stuff that helps me suck less.

As part of that search, I just signed an endorsement deal. While I shouldn't let my new sponsor's name slip, let me give you a hint: I've been bitten by the brand.

In my quest for less suckage, I've been fascinated by the proliferation of quite obviously useless devices that are touted as handicap-cutting miracles, and the apparently infinite number of people who buy them—golfers with too much money and not enough sense. Does anyone else remember the warm-up baseball-bat thingy with the water in it? If you could make it burp at the top of your backswing, you were in the perfect position.

My favorite at the moment is that hinged club, which when waved at the ball will either get you to the middle of the green with a birdie putt or to the emergency room with stitches in your lid. What a concept: Swing right or die.

I'm big into infomercials. There's one with me in it, looking like a tool-belted Turkish prison guard. I've been up and down five pants sizes and 11 hairstyles since that ad was made, but it's still running on The Golf Channel every time I turn on the telly. Granted, it's not as bad as the one in which Bobby Clampett flogs gas heaters for golf carts. Dear God, I wish I'd been in on the storyboards for that one: Let me see, let's take some propane, put it in a moving vehicle with Clampett, give him a box of matches, and dive for cover. *Cart rental: $32. Golf balls: $28. Greens fee: $85. Watching Bobby Clampett dive headfirst into a frozen lake because his hair is on fire: f---ing priceless.* Now that's a commercial.

The other one I love is for the Perfect Club. Peter Kessler who I believe is a 6-handicap vampire is perfect for the job. I once saw a shot of him on Golf Talk Dead, walking past a mirror with Phil Mickelson. For an instant, Phil was right-handed and Kessler was gone too weird.

So I'm thinking that if anyone out there wants to market a knockoff of the Perfect Club, give me a shout. I may not be perfect, but I think I'm quite good. So we'd call it the Quite Good Club, and it could be used from almost anywhere to do nearly everything. The Quite Good Club might not get you completely out of the bunker, but it'd certainly get you right up there under the lip. The concept might need work, but I think I'm on to something.

I've always fancied myself something of an ad exec. You know the type: ponytail and bowling shirt, brainstorming around the cube farm with a half-eaten cigar, and a crappy attitude. I would never have allowed Gary McCord to admit he plays with a soft noodle. And when Charles Howell III and Scott McCarron were hitting buttons in that elevator, why didn't David Duval walk in last and punch 59? Someone answer me that! And then this: When Johnny Miller said that great shots were "better against Jack," why the hell didn't someone punch *him*? We need more gratuitous punching in golf advertising, and more reality, too. If I see a fat, sign-carrying kid in shorts sneaking around the locker room, sniffing articles of clothing, I'd like to see Ernie Els and Jesper Parnevik ganging up and forcing his cheerful, chubby self into a locker.

I also think Frank the Headcover's eyes should pop out just a little now that Tiger's inserting a driver with a bigger head into him. That would have to sting a bit, no?

My favorite golf commercials are those with John Cleese, who is clearly over the Far Hills and far, far away. I couldn't watch that man open his eyes in the morning without bursting out laughing. But for sheer selling power, no one can compete with Tiger who, incidentally, learned how to act from McCord and me. You read it here first: The kid learned it all from us, on our Late Night Show, before he got famous and started buying watches with his AmEx and seeing dead people driving Buicks.

My 10-year-old son, Andrew, and I love your Cobra commercials; however, he is driving me crazy by repeatedly reciting the one where you express disdain for the term "nice ball." Also, we can no longer say "nice ball" to each other in earnest because in light of your commercial it sounds like a put-down. So I have two questions: How can I get him to stop imitating you and are there any other golf terms you intend to target?

— *Larry Levitt, Laguna Niguel, California*

Actually, I wanted to say, "Nice balls," but they wouldn't let me. To get young Andrew to stop imitating me, I will send you a CD-ROM of my most recent colonoscopy. Make him watch it over and over until he realizes that if he doesn't stop mimicking me, he may grow up to look just like it. I am currently evaluating new candidates for derision. They include: center cut, down the fall line, golf swing, golf ball, golf game, any description of a ball "chasing" somewhere, and pretty much anything uttered by Johnny.

The Fine Art of Ganching

You might remember that a while ago I told you I was going to Scotland and Ireland for a few days to play golf. I also said I'd keep a diary for you. Well, I lied. I didn't go to Scotland, I didn't play golf, and I didn't keep a diary. I did, however, go to Ireland, but the closest I got to playing golf was watching the World Match Play Championship on television.

We—my wife, baby girl, and I—flew from Dallas-Fort Worth Airport to Manchester, England last Tuesday and then on to sunny (not) Belfast, where I spent the entire week paddling furiously upstream against a steady torrent of Guinness. Frankly, I'm glad I only get to go back there once a year.

I have to say, though, there is something magical about watching golf on TV in a proper Irish Pub. It's exactly like being on the golf course, except you have a bar to lean against. I was in a lovely old Belfast bar called the Garrick, watching the Woosnam-Woods match last Friday, and was suddenly struck by the unusual attention span of the assembled crowd of good-natured ganches. A "ganch" is a term used to describe an extremely vocal Ulster person who mistakenly considers himself to be "an expert on most things." For instance, in Texas, Ross Perot would be a ganch, and I for one would pay a lot of money to listen to him after he'd had a skinful of Guinness. But I digress.

The ganching in the Garrick was going at a steady hum

while the players were between shots, then died to almost nothing when they addressed the ball, and rose again after the shot when the ball came to rest. It was pretty weird, to be honest, and made even weirder by the fact that the volume on the TV was turned all the way down. There must have been a hundred different conversations that kept coming to an abrupt halt every couple of minutes and then starting up again a few seconds later. Like I said, it was just like being on the golf course, except for all the smoke and the full bar service. Having said that, even the bartenders were afflicted. You could have danced naked on the bar during the playing of a shot, and you couldn't have gotten their attention either.

On Sunday, I watched the final from my parents' house, this time with the volume turned up. There was virtually no ganching. Well, except for my father, of course, and maybe me. Okay, definitely me, but my point is this: A bit of ganching, whether you agree with the gancher or not, makes golf watching more enjoyable, a phenomenon that the powers that be at CBS obviously noticed some time ago.

How many times have your heard "nice ball" since your commercial first aired?

> — *Mark, Grand Blanc, Michigan*

Counting your message, 4,625,989, which is good. Means I'm reaching the target demographic: 18- to 55-year-old unemployed drunks with incontinence issues who don't play golf, stayed at a Holiday Inn Express last night with a transvestite hooker suffering from self-image problems. Whoa, I've just described half the residents of Grand Blanc, which is where the Buick Open is played... I knew there was a reason I liked those people.

The Stupidity Channel

I thought of something earth-shatteringly brilliant the other day: my own television sports channel, dedicated to, and specifically for, idiots. And before you start yelling about how many of those are up and broadcasting already, take off your shorts, pal, soak them in brandy, wad them up, stuff them in your mouth, and light up that White Owl you've been saving, 'cause this one's for you!

I watch a lot of TV with my five children, and lately I've noticed an increase in moronic behavior for them to emulate. They don't need this because they have me. There's the snake guy for a start. I'm just waiting for the first lawsuit from the distraught parents of a toddler who thought it would be a good idea to tie a granny knot in a Western rattler.

Worse than that, this show has spawned a shoal of knockoffs, most of which seem to be hosted by escapees from Australian mental institutions who are intent on being bitten, mangled, mauled, or otherwise digested by a wide variety of creatures we used to teach our children to avoid. I told my kids that a snake bit me once, and it was very sore.

Call me an old stick-in-the-mud, but I think they should avoid sharks, too. But apparently, stupidity sells.

The idea hit me right after I watched that first XFL game, which was so magnetically unwatchable, it was impossible to stop watching. You know, in case something worse came on the screen. And then it did. The governor of the great state of Minnesota, followed by enormous, steamingly pneumatic, dentally magnificent, blonde cheerleaders, was introducing the players from the locker room. God, I love this country!

There was a guy on the field wearing a helmet, shooting huddle stuff with a mini-cam. If this were on CBS, I was thinking, the camera would be wearing the helmet. But also, I knew that somewhere, a lot of people were watching this, thinking it was cool.

This is my target audience! I work with a couple of people who are intelligent, have teeth, and cars that are all one color, and who like wrestling, for crying out loud. So, I figure just because I don't get it, doesn't mean it can't be gotten.

You see? I'm talking trailer trash already. This might begin to break ground for an experiment that could locate the extra chromosome that turns a mild-mannered bank clerk into a nutball who kicks a hole in his TV over a bad call in a greased midget-tossing bout. (They should have televised review of those things, anyway.) I want to give poor white trash, rich black trash, and all the other trashes in between, something to link hands over, and I want to hear them sing "Kumbayah," around the big screen.

The Stupidity Channel could create the human bridge that would link fans of the Westminster Dog Show and the Daytona 500. There's no reason why these people shouldn't mingle and perhaps even breed. I can see the scene at Hooters, as they pass around the wings and cucumber sandwiches: "C'mon, buddy, put the groundhog down an' givvus a big ol' hug... say, is that there feller in the sport coat an' beret sniffin' my wife's butt?"

The whole dog show thing is about the humans anyway. Not that there is anything wrong with living vicariously through your mutt, but it would be nice to see the judges rate the handlers and the dogs. Then, to find the best in show, they would add the scores together. On the Stupidity Channel, you'd see the elderly lady judge pulling back the lips of the handler of the Italian greyhounds to get a good look at his gnashers, and then plunging her hand into his pants. "Turn your head sideways and bark like a dog for me, sir."

Oh, yes, I could sell commercials on this network, I just know it. I'd buy "The Man Show" as well. The whole scantily clad girls on trampolines thing is a potential ratings monster, although I've found that to get a really good view, you need your own trampoline in the living room, and you have to time your bounce just right. It's a good idea to wear underwear, too, the gripper kind, or you might get a nasty whiplash.

There has to be a golf application, and McCord and I, who are the poster children for stupidity in broadcasting, intend to be in a position to capitalize from it. We could run promos for it during the XFL.

Who needs The Rock, when you have a genuine American legend in Gary McCord, who has also lost control of his eyebrows? Bring on the XGA. "EXTREME GOLF: NO RULES, NO DRESS CODE, AND TO HELL WITH PUTTING!"

I can hear him yelling it now, all dressed up in hiking boots, Bermuda shorts, a string vest, and a Prussian helmet, getting set to tee off. I rather fancy the old 1970s wrestling leotard look for myself, maybe with green Wellie boots, and a Kamikaze headband. No coin-toss for the honor, either—just tee it up, ten paces apart, and nail it at one another. First to flinch loses the tee.

We'd need nicknames on our shirts. He could be "Crazy But Senile, Too," and I could be "The Gasman Cometh." Each group would have its own walking announcer, who would rush in after every mistake and ask the player why it had happened. There would be no limit on the number of clubs, and no club would be illegal. There would be no free drops, but you could throw the ball as often as you wanted.

Balls in water hazards or deep brush and desert would have to be retrieved, and either thrown or played. This is where the snake and shark guys could be incorporated into the show.

Finally, after every round, the players would get to vote one competitor out of the tournament, including on Sunday, which would mean in order to win, you would have to finish second. Hey, the game was never meant to be fair. I read that somewhere.

We all have our opinions on what constitutes a sport, and the right to tune in to whatever we want. To me, watching a bunch of cretins ride mountain bikes down a near vertical ski slope is not entertainment, and neither is the XFL. Don't get me started on yachting, either.

The only way to make that activity interesting is with the yet-to-be-invented "Pirate-cam," which would show yachters being lashed to the mast with their trousers around their ankles, and their Rolexes being stolen. But witnesses to the same accident will tell different stories, depending on which side of the street they were standing at the time. We are all idiots, in one way or another, and we're all losers, too, except when we win, which is seldom. The only mistake we make is thinking we are in some way superior because of the sports that interest us.

My channel would be for the guy who has just returned home from a blind date that turned out to be his ex-wife. He could slump into his inflatable Bud Light armchair, flick on the box, and let his fevered mind cool.

Then, he could watch Winston Cup drivers doing their best to avoid the naked dog-wrestlers at Turn One, while in the infield, a team of paramedics are trying to pull the snake guy out of a 40-foot anaconda, all to the jubilant cheers of a crowd of third-graders and their parents.

The world would be an okay place again because he would feel coddled in the warm fuzzy blanket, gently thrown over him by his fellow morons. Try getting that kind of therapy from Dr. Laura, who would be on late morning, in the comedy section.

Normally when the clubhead strikes the ball, where should my waist/legs be? Facing the ball or already turning toward the target? What about my hands—in front or behind the ball?

— Mark, Marietta, Georgia

Good God, Mark, your swing must look like a strand of DNA! When the clubhead strikes the ball, it would be preferable if your waist and legs were still below your manly breasts, and at no time should your hands leave your wrists. However, your feet may occasionally disconnect from your ankles, but this is normal, and should be expected from time to time. It worries me that you don't seem to give a monkey's fart where your tongue is during this aberration. Where do you usually have it, molars, incisors, canine? Just have a lash at it, my boy, you're thinking way too much.

Terminal Logic

I'm thinking that it's been ages since I picked a good nit, so here we go. I, like many of you, watch a lot of sports on TV, and if there is one thing that I cannot stand, it's when an announcer assumes that his or her audience is unable to identify the sport that he or she is watching.

Here's an example. I'm watching Green Bay and Dallas try to severely injure each other on a big strip of grass, which is marked off in five-yard increments, and there is a set of goal posts at either end. The players are wearing body armor and helmets, and most of the crowd are wearing big lumps of cheese on their heads. The announcer says, "Brett Favre (and if that's pronounced, "Farve," then I've just farted) is in complete control of this football game, and is throwing the football with deadly accuracy."

Now, if I'm not mistaken, this is a GAME that is played with a BALL, and if there is anyone watching who has not yet noticed that it is a game called "FOOTBALL," then, to ensure the safety of us all, this person needs to be institutionalized as quickly as possible.

I, of course, use football as an example, but the problem is even more widespread in golf. The terms "golf ball, golf swing, golf shot, golf club" are all equally acceptable when used without being preceded by the word "golf," unless of course we start playing the game on a football field, or a hockey rink, and I don't see that happening any time soon. In fact, now that I come to think of it, hockey is thankfully one of the sports in which the announcers give the viewers the benefit of the doubt.

If Barry Melrose (who I think is the best analyst in any sport) ever says, "He shot that hockey puck so hard at Belfour," I shall feel as if someone has taken a swing at my balls. And I'm assuming you know which ones I'm talking about.

Four of us are playing golf in Ireland in August. Since we're closer to as old as God's dog than we may care to admit, we regularly visit trees along the fairway, as per the U.S. custom of purging last night's recreational beverages and today's coffee. Is such conduct acceptable on Irish courses? I don't mind being the "ugly American," and surely, wherever we are, we've been thrown out of worse. But I'd be loath to get the gate for avoidable stupidity; particularly if I happened to have parred a few consecutive holes.

— *Steve S.*

You and your pals could be in deep trouble. Where you're going to play, there are no trees. Hang it out wherever you want, but first check the area for sheep. Some of them can be very aggressive.

Don't Tell Me, You Have an Inner Ear Problem, Right?

The next time you are visiting an unfamiliar golf course, and some well-meaning local dolt tells you that, "everything breaks toward the ocean," or "toward the mountain," or anywhere else, I think you should ask them why they think that might be. If the answer is anything other than, "because the slope is that way," you need to thank them, and back away slowly.

I remember playing at the 1993 PGA Tour Qualifying School in Palm Springs, and being advised by one of the bag room guys that everything broke toward the town of Indio. The guy, whom I felt looked like an idiot savant type, wouldn't tell me in which direction Indio lay, but he told me that by the time I had played the course, I would have it figured it out for myself. He tapped the side of his nose, winked, took a swig from his Mickey's Big Mouth, and disappeared into the bag room.

After playing my first practice round, I deduced, in Galileo-like fashion, that the city of Palm Springs must be completely surrounded by Indio, which might well be a Native American word meaning "the rest of the United States." The guy wasn't an idiot savant, I thought, he was just an idiot. But later that same day I was out running on the streets around my hotel, when I witnessed two cars in a drive-by gun battle, after which both cars did indeed break toward Indio, so for a while there, I was a little confused.

I can't figure out why people believe that the ball can somehow be influenced by something other than slope, grain, or wind. I know the moon causes the tide to come in and go out, but how the hell are you supposed to know where the moon is in the middle of the day? I'm on my way back from Hawaii as I write, where I, like everyone except Brad Faxon, had a little difficulty reading the greens. You could hog-tie that boy, and he'd still make everything he looked at, probably with his nose. I have to be careful when I'm interviewing him, because if we look at each other at the same time, it looks like we're schnozzle fencing. His honker is bigger than mine, but I'm pretty sure I have him in that vital nostril-capacity department.

Anyway, I think my favorite red herring is the old ocean line. Virtually all the locals told me that the grain followed the sun, and everything sloped toward the sea. I told them that, considering how hot and bothered the grass must get after a day of sun-following, I was surprised that the whole golf course didn't take advantage of those wicked slopes and go for a wee swim every evening after sunset. That didn't go down too well.

I mean, for the most part, these are intelligent people (and presumably rotten putters), but it's not just in Hawaii that they reside. Take Pebble Beach for example. These poor Japanese duffers are paying four hundred bucks or whatever to play, for some cretin to tell them, in very slow, loud English, that, "EVERYTHING... BREAKS... TOWARD... THE... OCEAN." Then, they bow politely, and spend the next six hours watching 50 percent of the putts they hit break toward the Atlantic. It's a conspiracy, I tell you, but for some reason there are millions of willing participants. I feel it a duty, at the very least, to expose this evil plot and make a proclamation, so that the poor, duped, huddled masses may find some comfort in the truth, and finally come to believe in the great Isaac Newton. Here goes:

Dear Gravitationally Challenged Friends,

Bermuda grass grows in any direction it chooses. If you stand still on it for long enough, it will grow right up your you-know-what, taking over your body to such an extent that eventually you might have to fertilize your hair and mow your teeth. It follows water, slope, and good-looking women, and it does care about your ball, which often it will deliberately shove slightly uphill, just to screw with your mind, and make you believe the whacked-out dorkwit in the bag room.

Next, as no doubt most of you will already have noticed, once your ball has fallen into the hole, it will very rarely, if ever, fall out. For the same reason, an anvil, when dropped by the Roadrunner, will never shoot straight upward, decapitating the annoying, scrawny, honking little bastard. It always, always, plummets straight down, and lands right on top of Wile E. Coyote's head. It's called gravity, and it's also the reason we don't fall off the planet, which I'm led to believe is spherical, or pretty close to it.

So the next time anyone tells you that anything breaks anywhere, try hitting him or her with an anvil. If they fall up, you can call me down on the telephone and tell me that I'm a low-up, dirty rotten liar.

And another thing, if you're playing in Scotland and some wizened old caddie points a crooked finger in a field and says, "The sheep are lying doon, that means it's going to rain," remember where you are. You're in Scotland, and it's always going to rain. The sheep are lying down because they're either tired or dead.

David Feherty

David, why is it that the second one guy starts wearing his shades upside down on the back of his head, 50 follow suit the next day?

— *Chris Grzesik, Wadhurst, United Kingdom*

Because they all got a call from their agents the night before who said, "Listen, you morons, Titleist isn't paying your useless ass $100,000 to be on your headwear just so you can cover up their name with a pair of dopey-looking Oakley re-entry shields. Oakleys by the way, nimrod, isn't paying you s--t (and if they are, where's my 20 percent?) DON'T COVER UP THE LOGO, NUMB NUTS!!!"

The Root of All Evil

A thought struck me on the side of the head the other day and like most of the other ones, it bounced off harmlessly into my subconscious. The thing is, this one keeps bouncing back.

It appears to me that shortly after I quit playing competitive golf, the professionals started playing for a lot more money. It's probably a coincidence, but I have to admit I'm a little worried.

Call me old-fashioned (or insanely jealous), but I fear these newfound riches may lead those who love to play or watch our glorious game down the dimly lit and treacherous path that leads to the kind of behavior—both from players and fans—that plagues other, less noble pastimes. I'm sorry if that wasn't pompous enough for you, but it's the best I can do.

Actually, wait a minute. Maybe it isn't. Why, the pursuit of legal tender shouldn't be the motivating factor here. Surely we should strive to keep sacred those reasons that first lured most of us to the links. Like avoiding the car-pool line, the chance to lurk in a smoky bar telling lies when one's spouse is under the impression that one is engaged in a healthy pastime. And, of course, the opportunity to deliberately lose to someone whose business one's interest may be vested in.

Wouldn't you know it, but we're back to money again. I'm starting to understand how this happened. Perhaps it's just evolution, but even if it is, we must resist, for fear the entire species may mutate, given the dog-eat-dog nature of the game, into clones of either Donald Trump or Mother Teresa. Don't laugh. Think of the children.

I have personally witnessed the power that the mighty greenback can wield over those who are ill-prepared for the burden that comes with it. At the Sarazen World Open a couple of years ago, I had the responsibility of coaching a mild-mannered member of the public to make one attempt at a 25-foot putt for $1 million.

In front of cameras and a large crowd, I showed him the line and the speed, but when it came his turn, his every orifice dilated and his left wrist went into thermoplastic meltdown. This was no stroke; it was a heart attack.

We all know that money corrupts and Lord knows there's a lot of it in this country. In the five years I have lived here, up until now I have been reluctant to criticize American sports, mostly because I love nearly all of them—except basketball. Players sign $100 million contracts to put a ball through a hole in the air. That's too weird even for me. I firmly believe that every hole should have a bottom.

I remember watching my first college basketball game and being totally horrified by the fan behavior when one of the opposing teams stepped up to the free throw line. Everyone behind the basket started waving big wiggly things and shouting, "MISS! MISS! MISS!"

Speaking for myself, I've only done that once and that was in my third grade classroom. I was desperate for the bathroom.

Okay, I feel a rant coming on. Will someone please explain to me what this kneeling-down business at the end of a football game is about? Surely, you should be forced to play the ball. We're talking about men who play with the strength and courage of superheroes, unless they're a point in front with 60 seconds to go, in which case they fall on the ball like giggling girl scouts.

If you applied that rule to golf, instead of having to play the 72nd hole at Augusta, you could put the ball in your pocket and walk straight to Butler Cabin.

Growing up, I played rugby. I never got the chance to play either Gaelic football or hurling, although I did do my fair share of the latter after playing rugby. I've always enjoyed sports in which the object is to seriously injure your opponent while trying to avoid possession of the ball. At least that's the way I played. My golf looked much the same way, except the opponent I was trying injure was me.

The only violence you will see at a rugby match is on the field, which separates it from its much more popular rivals, soccer and Little League baseball. Rugby is a hooligans' sport played by gentlemen and soccer is, well, the other way around and the fans act likewise.

My problem with soccer is that the players cheat and this behavior has become an accepted part of the game. They dive after being tackled and claim possession of the ball no matter how obviously it belongs to the other team. Sort of like pro basketball, if you ask me.

Imagine these ethics in golf. You'd need a third pocket with a golf-ball-sized hole in it.

Golf is diametrically opposed to most other sports when it comes to crowd behavior because it's the events where no money is involved where we have the most trouble. The Ryder-Solheim Cup affliction seems to occasionally rob a player of his sense of fair play. I hope this doesn't creep into the game's mainstream because ugly crowd behavior usually follows ugly player behavior.

Players once cruised gracefully across oceans in steamships, giving lessons to elderly widows in between tournaments. They now whiz across the hemisphere in private jets and build golf courses while they chat on their cell phones during practice rounds, pausing only to relight their cigars.

That's why I've decided to rededicate myself and work tirelessly toward the salvation of what's left of our game before it's too late. I shall charge bravely at the enemy, thrusting my microphone right up the orifice of avarice and with my free hand I shall grab the gonads of greed.

While I live and breathe, the game of golf shall never be allowed to sink to the depths of these wars that used to be games, until we and television made them so life-and-deathly serious.

People seem to have forgotten for one reason or another that the pastime they're watching is meant to be a playful diversion— or fun, like a game, maybe.

If I should lose my battle, golf as we know it will be lost forever and I would surely find myself unable to do my job, my spirit broken, my life devoid of meaning.

Unless, of course, my game comes back around. In that case, to hell with the rest of you. I'm going for the gold.

Why are all of our older heroes always wearing sweaters in pictures from their glory days? The trees are in bloom and it looks hot out. Global warming?

— *Rick Stuckey, Mt. Prospect, Illinois*

You own that Stuckybowl joint where they film "Ed"? I love that place. They're wearing sweaters because the shirt companies wouldn't pay them then and the sweaters guys would. What gets done, Rick, is what gets rewarded.

A Goal and an Assist

I t's almost that time of year once more. Memories of winter are shrinking, but for me, I see only ice. That's right, it's almost time for the Stanley Cup playoffs. Regular readers know how much I love hockey, and that I have a few friends who play, or used to play. The great Ron Francis, Paul Coffey, Tony McKegney, to name a few... well, to name them all actually, or at least I thought so until just the other day, when I had to write a letter of apology to a player I've never even met. I'm talking about the Toronto Maple Leafs' Tie Domi.

Confused? Not as badly as I was, but the following letter to the NHL's version of the Tasmanian Devil is fairly self-explanatory:

Dear Tie:

As our mutual friend Tony McKegney may or may not have told you, I am an idiot.

However, my own tremendous standards in this area rocketed upward at a hell of a rate when, recently, I made the startling discovery that one of the signed photographs on the wall of my office was of you, and not (as I had thought for the previous year) of the aforementioned McKegney.

Now even by my standards, this is a staggering piece of stupidity, and for at least five reasons:

1.   The inscription on the photo reads, "To David, all my best, Tie Domi." (To some, this might have been a hint, although in my own defense here, you could be called for hooking, slashing, and offside for your signature, although it does appear possible that you might have been tripped in the act of writing it.)

2.   Tony McKegney is a big, bandy-legged black guy.

3.   You're not.

4.   You're insane.

5.   Okay, you got me on this one. Tony's insane too. To play hockey for a living, you have to be.

This whole sordid affair is made stranger still by the fact that McKegney and I are related. I have no idea how this happened, but until I met him, I thought I was black Irish. Anyway, he read in one of my pieces somewhere that I was interested in hockey, e-mailed me, telling me of the link between our families, and we became kind of online buddies. Tony is friendly with Mike Weir, and last year he came to the Masters. We arranged to meet in a bar behind the Augusta National. I still had no idea that he was black, but I spotted that, and the trademark Feherty/McKegney nose almost instantly the minute he introduced himself. I'm not THAT slow.

A friend of mine from Toronto was visiting me the other day, and he remarked upon your image, "Hey, nice photo of Tie Domi. I didn't know you knew him!"

I told him I didn't know Tie Domi, and that he was looking at a photo of Tony McKegney. "It's just a reflection off the ice, or a trick of the light or something," I muttered. But those Toronto people aren't so easily fooled. Most of the bastards know you.

Subsequently, Tony told me he had asked you to send the photo about a year or so ago, around the same time he had sent me one of himself, but he didn't realize that you had done so. Obviously he didn't tell me. I'm thrilled to have your picture on my wall though, and I wanted to write to thank you, and explain why my letter took so long! You must have thought I was a bigger asshole than I thought you were, and I was wrong about that. Since I've realized you are watching me as I write, I've taken the time to visit your website, and find out a little more about you. When you're not beating the crap out of adults, you manage to find the time to look after an enormous number of less than fortunate kids. Thanks for doing that, and thank you so much for signing and sending your photo to me. It's one that I will treasure.

Please accept a copy of my book, with kindest regards from one of your brethren. I'm sending you a photo, too, although it was taken from a strange angle, and I think it makes me look a little like Vijay Singh.

Good luck in the playoffs. Toronto has a new fan.

David Feherty

I enjoy your column and commentary—you have a great vocabulary and solid writing style. Having said that, I understand that you walked out of school at age 17, and your game benefited, I believe. My question is, did you ever go back and finish your education, and if so, where and when? If you quit school to better prepare for your golfing career, wouldn't it make sense to finish school to better prepare you for your current one?

— *Derek, Charlotte, North Carolina*

Derek: What a great name. I always wanted to be named after something made with girders and I-beams and stuff. Did my dad put you up to this? No, I did NOT finish my formal education. You have a problem with that, huh? If I've done as well as I have without an education, how much better could I have done with one? Not much, I think. I'm not against education, I just knew what I wanted to do and did it. When I was 28, my dad asked me if I was ever going to go back to and get a degree. I said it would take five or six years and what the hell was the point of having a degree at that age? He said, "Well, how old will you be in five or six years if you don't get a degree?" The problem is, I'm not educated enough to understand what he meant.

Dudley vs. Snidely

You have no doubt noticed upon the cover of this rag that sugary piece of do-goodery about how a person might gain fair advantage or "edge" over his or her opponent.

Well, Dudley Do-Right, if that's how you want to go about it, just make sure you save some tea and crumpets for me down at the yacht club afterward.

This month, my name is Whiplash, pal, as in Snidely. The way I see it, most of us who play do so with little or no regard for the Rules, anyway. If you're going to do it wrong, you might as well get it right and include a decency bypass as well.

Over the next few minutes, I'm going to give you a crash course in how to cheat and weasel your way into your hapless opponent's hip pocket, so prepare yourselves. These are some of the most dastardly deeds in golf, and although I would never recommend using such techniques in competitive play, that's exactly where most of them have their roots. Over the last 20 years or so, I've bumped into a few rogues and villains who were perfectly happy to make up for their lack of talent on the links with either sleight of hand or nudge of foot.

First, Snidely says it's always a good idea to get his opponent in a bad mood, and preferably before a ball is struck in anger. While they're in the locker room lacing up, Snidely makes a small bet that is designed to make our hero, Dudley, feel like an idiot. He takes the newspaper off the table and says, "I bet you five bucks that if we both stand on this paper face to face, you can't knock me off it with your best push."

Dudley, of course, senses evil afoot, but try as he may, he can't see how the hell Snidely could manage to stay on the paper, even if given only a moderate shove. "You're on!" he says.

Snidely then marches into the bathroom and spreads the paper on the floor, half in, half out of one of the stalls. "Stand on it then," he says with an obsequious smirk. Dudley obeys. Snidely stands up, shuts the door to the stall, and stands on the other half of the paper. Their eyes meet over the top of the door. "Push away," says Snidely.

Dud's one down and they haven't reached the first tee yet. When they do get there, Dud is given the honor, and while he is bending down to tee his ball up, Snidely surreptitiously picks up the nearside tee marker and replaces it a little farther back so it seems that Dud is teeing off from in front of the markers. If Dudley hits a good one, Snidely will ask him to play again. Snidely issues an evil chuckle, and the match is under way.

Snidely has a pocket full of greenish-brown markers, which he has little or no intent to use. On the first green, he pretends to mark his ball, but keeps the marker in his fingers as he picks up the ball. Then he waits for Dudley to putt. While Dud's ball is on its way to the hole, Snidely replaces his ball some six feet closer to the hole, and makes a display of putting his marker back in his pocket. Again, Dudley smells something, but has no evidence of foul play. (I know of one player who actually did this for years before being caught.)

Snidely is wearing a pair of snow-white golf shoes, and by the next tee, he has figured out the extent of Dudley's peripheral vision as he addresses the ball. Snidely makes sure his feet are just in view as Dudley starts his backswing, and Snidely moves his right foot about four inches closer as Dudley gets to the top. This often causes a player to flinch, and better still, to look for the move on the next shot. Of course, Snidely never does it again. Or does he?

Occasionally during the round, Snidely offers sycophantic praise to Dudley. Snidely shamelessly brown-noses about how beautiful Dudley's balance is and how elegant his swing. "Oooh, that was a beauty!" says Snidely of Dudley's tee shot, as it comes to rest 20 yards behind his own.

Snidely's next dirty deed is performed on a hole where both tee shots finish out of view, perhaps over a ridge or around a dogleg. Whenever Dudley hits the longer tee shot, Snidely compliments him on the size of his equipment, his undeniable manliness, or such. This time when both balls are hit on a similar line, Snidely makes sure he gets off the tee quicker than Dud and makes it to his ball first.

Upon reaching his tee shot, Snidely gives it a cursory glance and then a dramatic double take. Then saying, "Mother of Pearl, but I must have hit a real snot-squirter there!" he strides proudly forward to Dudley's ball, plumps down his bag beside it, and turns to wait for Dud. The worst that can happen here is that Dudley will notice the error and call Snidely back to his own ball, in which case he will say, "Silly me," and play on.

Dudley, of course, is a zoned-out turnip, and he goes right

ahead and hits the wrong ball. Naturally, it's a beauty, and Snidely is lost in admiration. Then, as Snidely gets into his final waggle, he is dramatically struck by the ghastly realization that this is not his ball. "Ahem," he says, somewhat embarrassed. "That'd be my hole, I believe."

It's cold, the match is all-square on the final hole, and Snidely has been waiting for it to start raining before he pulls his next fast one. He's in luck, 'cause a chilly drizzle starts to fall and he and his dozy opponent are just off the edge of the green. Snidely seems a little put off by the not-particularly-close proximity of Dudley's ball. He asks Dudley to mark it, which of course he is perfectly entitled to do.

Because it's wet and a little nippy, too, Dudley sticks a tee in the ground behind his ball, lifts it, and like most of us would, shoves his hands in his pockets. Brrrrr… (Buzzer, please.) This is not allowed under the Rules of Golf, which state that a ball off the putting surface that has been marked and lifted is not allowed to be cleaned, unless there is a drop involved. When you slip it into the lint, you are deemed to be cleaning it. Oh, dear, what a pity. "My hole," says the evil one, and the match is over.

However, upon doing the gentlemanly thing and striding manfully over to shake the cold, limp hand of his sneaky foe, Dudley goes a little out of his way to notice a short, cut-down putter, which has been hiding beneath the lip of Snidely's golf bag since Dud (who apparently isn't as daft as he looks) cunningly placed it there before they teed off.

As usual, good prevails over evil, and Dudley rides off into the sunset with the beverage-cart girl.

My Career High

D

ear Ron:

Sorry it has taken so long for me to reply, but McCord made me write replies to both fan letters he received this year before he let me out from under his desk. It was either that or "deal with the cigar thing," whatever that means.

Anyway, with regard to the best shot I ever hit, there is one that kind of sticks in my memory and I will do my best to describe it for you. I say, "do my best," because to be perfectly honest with you, to this day I'm not sure if the whole episode wasn't a figment of my imagination. The shot itself was real, and that's a fact, but whether or not it looked the same to the crowd as it did to me is another story.

It was the final of the 1990 Dunhill Cup, which was in effect the three-man team championship of the world and yours truly was, through no fault of my own, the gallant skipper of the Irish side. My two teammates were Ronan Rafferty and Philip Walton, and we were up against the old enemy, the English.

The event was played in October over the hallowed turf of the Old Course at St. Andrews, and on our way to the final I'll be damned if I can remember which teams had the decency to lose to us, but I'm fairly sure some of them must have been communists. As captain, I had chosen to play in the last of the three matches and was drawn against my friend, the veteran Ryder Cupper and formidable match player, Howard Clark.

Now, I'm not proud of this bit, but these were different times, and even though there was a lot of money at stake, it was still considered silly season. And I was considered silly. Anyway, that day I teed off with what Saddam Hussein might have called "The Mother of All Hangovers."

Had it not been for the kindness/bigotry of the Scottish spectators, it was a match I surely would have lost. You have to understand that after the Scots are knocked out of any team event in any sport, they will instantly become rabid supporters of anyone who is playing the English. That's just the way it works.

Now as I mentioned, I wasn't feeling exactly spiffing, and subsequently—after a dozen or so holes of medal/match play, some blundering, and one near fall into one of the Coffins—I found myself a couple back of Howard. Trust me, in professional golf, there is no worse feeling than to hit a three-foot putt so fat that the bastard finishes short of the hole. But then, as I made my way from one green to the next tee, in an Elijah-and-the-chariot-of-fire-descending-from-the-heavens kind of way, a shiftless, tweedy-looking sort in the crowd made contact with me.

Don't ask me where it happened, because I can't remember. St. Andrews is a magnificent enough illusion at the best of times, but when you can't tell whether you're blown up or stuffed, it's like a day-trip into golf's hall of mirrors. (By the way, I've always wanted to rename the hazards at St. Andrews. Screw the principal, and his nose too. I mean, what kind of a nose has only one nostril?)

"Hey, Jimmy!" this idiot hissed (for that is the customary way to hail a stranger in Scotland). "Ye look like ye might need a wee biff on the magic bongwater!"

I glanced over at the crumpled overcoat of a man with an impossibly small head, crowned by, of all things, an Oakland A's baseball cap. With skeletal fingers, the wee man was clutching a dirty pewter hip flask to his chest, as if it contained a genie of some kind. He was grinning broadly, displaying a mouth full of broken china, and his eyes were closer together than a racing dog's balls. The right shoulder of his coat was shiny and worn, so instantly I knew he was a caddie, and a lifer at that.

"Aye, go awn," said his gormless pal, who had a face like a half-chewed caramel, looked equally lit, and had the demeanor of someone who might just have a betting slip favoring the Micks about his dingy person.

I stopped, and hesitated for about a millisecond, which was about an hour longer than needed to get the crowd involved. I was going to look like a fairy if I didn't take a hit on the flask. Accompanied by a few hoots, at least one holler, and an indeterminate number of slaps on the back, I threw a good swallow down my neck and spent the next few minutes trying to cough up an internal organ. In certain parts of Scotland, the locals still make their own firewater, which is then covertly distributed in unlabeled whiskey bottles. (They don't have to tear off the old label, because as soon as the bottle is refilled, it jumps off by itself.)

I don't know what the stuff was, maybe some kind of industrial cleaning product, but I couldn't speak for about four holes. It had the unfortunate side effect of making the entire golf course seem somewhat mauve, but boy did it straighten me up. I played like a man possessed, and by the time I'd signed my scorecard, I'd halved the match, and the final was tied. To decide it, Howard and I had to play a sudden-death playoff.

My two caddie pals were waiting for me at the edge of the practice green before I teed off, and once more I felt it best to comply with their instructions. After all, they seemed to know how to get a man around St. Andrews. Howard and I halved the first two holes, but as fate would have it, this trip would end on the next, the legendary Road Hole.

I stood on the tee, gazing at the building in front of me with its famous lettering emblazoned across the wall: "Old Course Hotel." I hadn't a clue what line to hit my tee shot on, and was waiting for the ground to stop moving so I could tee up my ball, when, sensing my confusion, Harry, my faithful sack-dragger, muttered out of the corner of his mouth, "Hit it at the 'F' in Hotel."

I looked at him, then back at the letters on the wall.

"Harry," I said, "there is no 'F' in Hotel."

Harry looked at the ground, shaking his head. "No, no, no, you idiot," he hissed under his breath. "I said hit it at the EFFING hotel."

"Oh yeah," I nodded. "I thought that's what you meant."

So I hit it at the effing hotel, and the right-to-left wind drifted the ball back to the left edge of the fairway. Howard missed the fairway left, then pulled his second way left of the green, leaving his ball with one of the world's most impossible chip shots, from behind the ghastly little toilet bowl known as the Road Bunker. This was my chance. One good swing, a high draw with a 3-iron, land the ball on the little nasal outcrop at the front of the green/mauve, and let it run up toward the back lip and hope the slope takes it around behind the hole.

I'd love to say I remember the swing, but I don't. I swung, it flew, and suddenly it got deafeningly quiet in my head. I do, however, have a lasting image of the ball, hung up in a sepia sky, drifting past the cherry-picker camera and descending dream-like down in front of the backdrop of the crowd in the bleachers behind the road. As the ball landed on the front of the green, people began to stand up. Carried back to me by the breeze, the roar began to build, and the silence was gone.

Like the undertow from a Mexican wave, the crowd noise sucked the ball toward the back edge of the green, perilously close to the little lip over which lies the tarmac road and the dreaded limestone wall, and then it gently blew my little egg back down and around behind the flagstick, where it nestled about 15 feet from the hole. Two putts from there, and I had won the Dunhill Cup for Ireland, on the most famous hole on the most famous course in the world.

It is a moment that no one will ever be able to take away from me, largely because even I don't know where I put it.

They gave each of us a nice trophy and I don't know where that is either, but I do remember filling it with something special that evening and passing it around in the lobby of the Old Course Hotel. Hey, trophies are overrated anyhow, because unlike memories, they gather dust and can't be embellished. Everyone in the lobby of the Old Course Hotel saw mauve that night, and the last thing I remember was the overcoat and his pal, hand in hand, skipping across the 17th green toward the Auld Gray Toon.

The shot I hit that day is special to me because of the stage and the cast of characters involved. The Old Course is a whisky-soaked cathedral, the caddies are its clergy, and for me its most sacred ground is the Road Hole, with that green which can be either high altar or sacrificial pedestal, depending on the journey you take to get there, and what it does to your mind along the way. Even if it's not green, it'll grow on you.

I was watching The Golf Channel the other day, and they showed the highlights from the 1991 Ryder Cup. You actually won a couple matches, eh? You looked young, fit and like you knew what you were doing on the golf course. My God, man, what the hell happened?

—— *Zack Stevens, Shrewsbury, Massachusetts*

That wasn't me. The Golf Channel knew this all along. They called me for a comment on what appeared to be some kind of cloning experiment that went horribly wrong. I tried to explain that it was a different David Feherty, but they were having none of it. I'm in the process now of suing The Golf Channel for slander, libel, misrepresentation, rape, sodomy, bestiality, malfeasance, character assassination, and intestinal gas. Oh, don't you worry, they're gonna pay, all right. When I'm through with them, they'll wish they had never HEARD of David Feherty.

What a Day That Was

I quit playing competitive golf right about the same time that Tiger Woods turned pro. Coincidence? I think not. Hey, like I say, people hate me because I'm lucky. A week ago on Monday, however, I did play against Tiger for the first time, in a charity skins match to benefit the Shriner's hospital in New Bern, N.C. It is an event that has been hosted for the last 11 years by Sarah and Curtis Strange (in Sarah's hometown) and this year the participants were Curtis, Justin Leonard, Tiger, and I. Spot the odd man out in that group.

As little golf as I play these days, I thought it might be a good idea to hit a few balls the week before—you know, to see which barrel it was coming out of. So I zipped up to Royal Oaks, where Justin's coach, Randy Smith, manhandled my seized-up setup and swing into something less unsightly. A hell of an achievement. Of course, the next day I couldn't get out of bed. I should have known better than to wake up dead muscle tissue.

By Sunday, travel day, I was raring to go, though, and I flew from Dallas to Raleigh, where I waited three hours to catch a crop-sprayer to New Bern. One seat on the left, two on the right, and the plane was full. Thirty minutes later, joined at the hip and shoulder, my new best friend and I tore apart, and I stumbled out curbside to meet my limo.

No limo. So I call Curtis, who tells me there is a limo, and it's there, and the driver is looking for me. I tell Curtis there isn't, it's not, and he's not looking very hard. I give Curtis a description: I'm wearing green Airwalks, skateboard shorts, a long-sleeved T-shirt, and four days of beard. Think elderly Bart Simpson, with a worse attitude.

Ten minutes later, a car and driver, both of which have been waiting over at the private field, show up. They thought I had a jet, like the other three. Perfectly understandable. So I get to the hotel, get into my room, and then go and kick the doors of the other three, and run back inside. Also perfectly understandable. Then, I fill in my breakfast order—two eggs (slightly on the sunnyside-up side of over-medium), bacon, sausage, hashbrowns, a toasted bagel with cream cheese, coffee, and Tabasco on the tray, please—and I hang it on my doorknob. Leonard, the turd, who is right across the hall from me, is watching through his pinhole. And when my door closes, he sneaks out, and replaces my card with one from his room. In the morning, I am awakened approximately two hours earlier than necessary, and served a box of All-Bran, two cans of Lima beans, and a Bud Light. I can hardly contain my mirth.

Hmm, I'm thinking. There could be a way to turn this to my advantage. So I eat about half the box of All-Bran, chug one of the cans of beans, drain the beer, and go back to sleep. About an hour later, a very loud noise wakes me once more, followed by my alarm call. I was ready.

At the press conference, Curtis, the host, gets to choose his partner. He chooses me. Everybody can hardly contain their mirth. Bearing in mind that this man is your Ryder Cup captain, I feel that this does not augur well for the Belfry. A minor misjudgment perhaps.

To make a long and humiliating story short and humiliating (despite some elderly gamesmanship and cunning, and plenty of magnificently timed strategic flatulence), we got our butts kicked. Also, my evil plan backfired on me when I had to make a panic-stricken bathroom visit to a private house just off the 16th tee. We were all live-miked to a mobile PA system. I would have gotten away with it, if it hadn't been for the acoustics in the bathroom.

It was so much fun, I could not adequately explain it to you. They made a lot of money for sick and injured children, some of whom were there. Tiger, who had just won the Bell Canadian Open the day before, signed about a million autographs, had 70 group photographs taken, and gave me his cold. Justin was equally brilliant with the huge crowd, always giving, always smiling. Somewhere down the road, I am going to crazyglue his shoes together. Sarah and Curtis, one of the tour's great love stories, were the people who made it happen, and when the poster child for the event—a smiling little girl also called Sarah—walked out on her new prosthetic legs, all beautiful, and brave, and broken, I felt like hugging them both.

I got to play with Curtis Strange, Justin Leonard, and Tiger Woods, and I got a T-shirt with their names on it, and mine too!

What a day that was.

A few of us were recently discussing our dream foursome. Mine included Jack Nicklaus (because he is the best ever), Tiger Woods (in case I'm wrong about Jack), and David Feherty (because I'd like to beat one of them). Who is in your dream foursome?

— *Colin King, Saskatchewan, Canada*

Uh-huh Collywobbles. It's definitely a dream if you think you can beat any of those three, including me. Just because I don't play anymore doesn't mean I'm not still majestic. I know there's not a lot to do in Saskatchewan (which, by the way, is Indian for "don't put your tongue on the pump handle"), but you may want to lay off the pepperoni before bedtime. My dream foursome would be: Richard P. Feynman, the Nobel Prize-winning physicist who discovered quantum mechanics (there's some stuff I want to go over with him); then there's Sir Herbert Turdflurry, the inventor of modern underpants; and of course Rosie O'Donnell, who scares the living s--t out of me. Ideally, we'd go to the practice green, she'd hit a few putts, then I'd run away, skipping the golf altogether.

Practice Blows

I vaguely remember the range. In my brief prime, if a player spent three hours on the range after his round, maybe 30 minutes would be spent hitting balls. The rest was frittered away playing grab-ass, telling jokes, releasing stunt flatulence, fiddling with new clubs, watching other players hit balls and generally trying to find any excuse not to hit any yourself. Players would cosy up behind anyone who was actually trying to work, either to poke fun at him or to toss in their two cents' worth of genius.

Nowadays, the range is a row of much grimmer professional athletes, plus superstar coaches who pinch off mean little loaves of inaudible encoded information for their protégés. Not that there's never any fun out there. Finding the electronic controls to the irrigation system and setting off the sprinklers is always a lark, and who wouldn't enjoy being goosed by Sergio Garcia? But it's not like it used to be.

Dear God, I'm starting to sound like every old fart who ever wrote about the good old days. Maybe it's because I never really understood the kind of pervert who actually *enjoys* practicing. Because the fact is, practice blows.

Of course, I am from a place that was hardly ideal for honing a young man's game. The practice area at Bangor Golf Club in Ireland was a tiny mudflap wedged between the ninth and 18th holes. I'd dump a shag bag of chopped-up Dunlop 65s and begin irritating grumpy old members who sliced and hooked their way into the shabby pattern of dung-encrusted pills I sprayed in front of me. Vijay Singh wouldn't have lasted 10 minutes at Bangor—they'd have tossed him out on his ear for some grass-ackward turf violation.

Back then, hitting balls before a round was almost unsportsmanlike, and for a *child* to do it was evidence of bad parenting. But things were different in America—by the time Davis Love III was a tyke, his dad was parking a golf cart by a green so little DL3 could practice pitches. "Under the steering wheel!" DL2 would shout, or "Over the roof!" and the Lovelet would adjust his ball position and setup to hit the shot. Which was nothing like my own experience. My father would park himself on a stool in the men's bar while I was out practicing, and he'd shout to the bartender, "I'll have one more, Jimmy, and then I'll stay."

Today, alas, I am sore from *not* hitting balls. All those muscles I once used every day are thrust into violent action about once a month, and then spend the next month recovering from the shock. Maybe that's why Vijay keeps hitting balls long after the next-to-last player leaves the range. He's afraid to stop. Hours later, under cover of darkness, Joey the trainer leopard-crawls onto the range, heaves Vijay over his shoulder and sneaks him into his room through the fire escape at the hotel. Because golf is like a lot of schedule-3 drugs: You have to ease your way off. Vijay can't even stop when he gets back to his room. It takes several hundred short swings with the weighted stick and a CD soundtrack of tearing Velcro to bring him down so he can go out for dinner. Even then, you can be sure that if a pea ends up in his mashed potatoes, whoever ordered the calamari rings can expect some kind of miniature explosion shot, played toward his plate with a modified fish knife.

Vijay Singh will force you to have an opinion of him. Some say he's overly cool and standoffish, but my theory is that shooting people the bird is just his way of saying, "Have a nice day." He may not have much time for the media, but the hardest worker ever—he makes Ben Hogan look like Fred Couples— always has time for his fellow players. He's a throwback that way, and maybe the greatest compliment I can offer him is to say he reminds me of Payne Stewart, always willing to watch and offer tips to anyone who asks.

Vijay's legendary practice sessions aren't just mindless nut-crushing, either. He'll hit bags and bags of full shots from fairway bunkers, just to ensure he makes perfect contact. Christy O'Connor, Sr., used to do something like that—he'd hit so many drivers off the beach at Royal Dublin that you could have shaved with the baseplate on his wooden driver—but even he took a break now and then to go to the bar. Vijay just keeps on swinging, swinging, swinging. And getting better. That's bad news for the guys spending extra hours on the range to keep up with him, but hey, it leaves more room at the bar for the writers.

A science question: I've heard that a frozen golf ball loses 20 percent of its bounce. Can you confirm this? When "thawed" does it regain all its bounce again? I store my clubs in the garage over the winter (it freezes here in Minnesota) and now wonder if it has been affecting the performance of my golf balls.

— *Steve in Minnesota*

Thank God you told me you were from Minnesota, otherwise I would have thought you were just deranged. I've come to expect this sort of question from people from Minnesota who seem to focus enormous amounts of intellectual energy on issues surrounding their freezing balls. Can't say as I blame them.

Your golf balls are definitely affected by temperature during the winter. Here's what I would recommend. About mid-March (March 17th is a good target date), gather all your golf balls from the garage. Wash them. Take them to your local bar. Order an empty beer pitcher and two bottles of Black Bush. This is an Irish whiskey made in Northern Ireland and possesses extraordinary curative capabilities. Place the balls in the pitcher and fill the pitcher with enough whiskey to cover the balls. Swirl the balls around in the whiskey for a couple of minutes. Use a swizzey stick if you want. Do not add ice to this mixture under any circumstance; these balls have been through enough. Gather some friends from the bar around; you'll need them soon enough. After about 20 minutes in the Black Bush, strain the balls from the whiskey and dry them off carefully on a clean terry cloth towel. Drink the whiskey straight up from shot glasses with your friends until exhausted or drunk. Then take the balls out into the alley and set them on fire and never use them again, because they're worthless and always were. Give up golf and take up windsurfing.

Abducted by Aliens

Okay, I've got a good news/bad news story for you. After the five-hole playoff last week at the John Deere Classic, your sweat-soaked course reporter here scurried to the Quad Cities airport and barely made a flight to Seattle. I was headed for the Fred Couples Invitational at the spectacular new Newcastle Golf Club in Bellevue, Washington.

I got in around 1:30 in the morning, still damp and probably pungent, and polished off a bottle of red wine and a pizza with my old friend and coach Mike Abbott, who is the Director of Golf at Newcastle. I went to bed, and then a strange thing happened: I was abducted by aliens, and returned a few hours later. I only remember it vaguely, but I know it happened because the next morning I got up, went to the golf course, shot 66, and tied with Scott McCarron for the lead. There were 20 tour pros playing and I was in front of all of them but one. I had obviously been significantly interfered with during the night.

Still, I might as well have a good old gloat over my new-found proficiency, I thought, so I set about verbally abusing the likes of Stadler, Calcavecchia, Jacobsen and, of course, Freddie. I MC'd the evening function and made sure that everyone respected my authority. I was, of course, aware that the reverse gloat was probably just around the corner.

Actually, the reverse gloat didn't even have the decency to

hide around the corner: it was waiting for me on the first tee the next morning. My caddie, Dutch Skiver, a well-known Seattle idiot who was employed for entertainment value, handed me the 3-wood which I hit a hundred yards left, never to be seen again. I started with a couple of sixes and then fell away a bit. Dutch was looking at me in that "Who the hell are you?" kind of way, so I explained to him that I felt the effects of the suppository the little green men had given me had worn off. I followed my 66 with a 77. I'm glad it was only two rounds, because I'm pretty sure I didn't have a 55 in me.

While I have always liked your commentary on the course, I have been really impressed with your knowledge of the trees. Instead of saying, "He has to get over that big tree on the corner," you'll actually identify exactly what kind of tree it is. Where did you learn that?

—*Tom Timmons, Woodland, Washington*

When I was playing, I spent most of my time in the woods. I adore trees. They're like relatives to me (except trees are smart and I like them).

I Swooned at Troon

Ah, the open championship is back in bonnie Scotland. The name of the game, where the skirl of the pipes and the sweet bleat of a nice wee sheep can put a tilt in yer daddy's kilt. Lovely biscuits! Royal Troon was the site of my first and best chance to win the oldest major of them all, and I couldn't have choked harder if I'd been swallowing Donald Trump's hair.

The night before, I had seen my name spelled incorrectly on the giant, piddle-yellow scoreboard at the 18th—me, within striking distance of the lead!—and the shock had settled in for the evening. Believe me, sports fans, I knew I wasn't good enough to win a major. So I had no choice. I had to avoid accidentally getting so close that I'd have to bugger something up spectacularly toward the end and look like a total Van de Velde.

I was a *normal* tour player, not one of those freaks who live on adrenaline, hammering in three-footers for par all day like they're as relevant as Ricky Martin's girlfriend. Putts that mattered terrified me. On every one, I was so clenched you could have held me by the ankles and used my butt cheeks to cut the wires on the Golden Gate Bridge. And so my wins were in the minors, and after each one I would go deep the other way. A Feherty victory was always followed by months of anticlimactic, postorgasmic mediocrity. Until I needed money again. If my career were a song it would be Tom Waits's

"Emotional Weather Report": *"High tonight / Low tomorrow / And precipitation is expected."*

Broke, I would panic and set about eating All-Bran, practicing, running and, as a last resort, begging the Almighty for forgiveness. (Funny enough, that last trick always worked.)

So there I was at Troon in '89, drawn with Mark Calcavecchia in the last round, and as luck would have it, the idiot's zipper was at half-mast on the 1st tee. As usual, he looked like a human laundry basket. What chance had an ugly American, here at this sacred golfing mecca nestled between the edge of runway zero-niner at the Prestwick airport and a trailer park full of bluish-white people who eat their young? (Why are most of Britain's and Ireland's great courses bordered by bluish-white-trash trailer camps?)

I, on the other hand, was magnificent—slim, tanned, tailored and, with four large brandies cunningly concealed in two cups of coffee at lunch, hardly even shaking. I was ready to instigate my cunning plan: I reckoned I would stay in contention until we reached the Postage Stamp, where Sarazen made 13 back in 1426, or Weiskopf went elk-hunting or something, and where I could feasibly take a large number and still look windswept and utterly heroic as I limped heartbroken into the canyon of the last hole. "Had it not been for the dreaded eighth hole," Peter Alliss would say between sips of Bollinger, "the bold Ulsterman might have been Open champion."

Which, as Peter knows better than most, would have been bollocks. Truth is, I *thought* I wanted to win the Open in '89 and again in '94, but when it came down to it (just like Jean Van de

Velde) I didn't want the responsibility. There must have been a pivotal putt or shot, but I don't remember missing it. I do know I wasn't brave or dumb enough to stay in contention and then flop at the 18th. That could ruin a man for life.

Open champions are men like Greg Norman, Nick Price, Ernie Els and Calcavecchia, who played the last six holes that day like a man possessed by the opposite of whatever it was that had me by the throat. He hit a driver from the bony fairway of the par-5 16th to the heart of the green, a shot like nothing I'd ever seen. He hit an 8-iron from the rough at the last that landed by the flagstick like a sack of spuds, making the old farts in the bay window spill their gin and tonics and start squealing about square grooves. He knocked in the putt for three, then went out and won a playoff with Norman and Wayne Grady. I had no business being near that.

If my career were a poem, I'd want it to be Seamus Heaney's "Digging." Heaney told of how his father and grandfather dug potatoes from the ground. *"I've no spade to follow men like them,"* he wrote. *"Between my finger and my thumb / The squat pen rests. / I'll dig with it."*

I've no clubs to swing with men like the Open champions, but I have these words. So I'll swing away with them and be happy.

Your "I Swooned at Troon" article is perhaps one the most insightful I have ever read. It works on so many levels: humility, humor, insight, anthropological, psychological, sociological, entomological, herpetological... All right, the last two don't count, and I'm exerting too much effort, but let me end by saying, my man, you're not half bad.

— Ed

Whoaaaa, hold on now there, podner. Way too many logicals in there. I'm not smart enough to figure out that many angles simultaneously or even at the same time. Appreciate the credit, though. I'll keep writing as long as you keep reading. Thanks.

Right Club, Wrong Player

OK, so McCord shoots 7-under-par for the Bank One Championship last week in Dallas, and even if he had putted badly he could have finished second behind Watson. A badly injured hamster would have made more birdies off the second shots McCord hit over the three days. I hate to admit it, but he is a very good player indeed. More to the point, I am, as I found out, a very average caddie. He could have gotten better advice from the cart I was driving. Thanks to that cart, though, I was able to comply with half the instructions I was given on the first tee, those being, "Keep up and shut up."

You could be forgiven for thinking that, given the amount of time I spend with great players and their caddies, I should have some idea when to take the flagstick and when to shut my cakehole, but you'd be wrong. I had way too much attitude to be a good caddie. Whenever Gary hit it into a bunker, I'd be there with a couple of sand wedges, the putter, and a rake at the ready, with a damp towel slung over my shoulder. After he splashed out, I raked the bunker, invariably dropping the towel in the sand, and then rushed over to swap the sand wedge for the putter, take the flagstick, and clean the ball the same time. I looked like a monkey standing up in a hammock, making love to a set of bagpipes.

Only once in three rounds did he tell me he hit the wrong club. Instead of acting like a good caddie and taking my lumps, however, I told him it was the right club and he was the wrong player. After the last round I stood with him, signing autographs, and it struck me why Fluff got into trouble. Also, I realized that I probably had more fun than any other caddie in the tournament, and that I was definitely the only caddie that got paid exactly what he was worth. Zero.

David, do you and Gary McCord ever play against each other and who often wins? (Note: I hesitated before typing the "who wins" part because I can guess the answer.

— Kevin, Atlanta, Georgia

We try desperately to avoid playing on the same planet together, let alone on the same golf course. Actually, no, we don't play together at all if we can avoid it. I can't stand to see him mincing around, listen to him sigh and cluck when he misses his 45th putt of the day, constantly yakking on the cell phone to one of those Hollyweird producers about some hair-brained, stupid, half-baked golf sitcom, while all the while waving at a "so five minutes ago" celebrity while simultaneously muttering under his breath what a loser the guy is. This is not my idea of fun golf. And I have never lost to him.

Trophy Cases

I'm sitting at my desk, staring out through the oak shutters at the rain pelting down outside my window. It's one of those violent summer mornings, and a line of thunderstorms is barging through the Dallas area, tearing at the treetops, washing the streets clean of dust, and tangling the storm drains with twigs and leaves.

My office is oak paneled, and at the moment it's so dark that I've had to turn on the lights so I can see the letters on my keyboard. Unlike some of the writers in this rag, such as the evil Strange, I am not blinded by the glare of silver and gold from a vast array of glowing winner's buckets. Just a few moments ago, Rory, my youngest son, came in and asked if it would be okay if he took my Scottish Open trophy upstairs. Apparently he and his brother, Shea, are playing hoops with a Ping-Pong ball, and the trophy is about the right size to serve as the basket.

Whatever. My cohort McCord blotted his magnificent losing record once he got to the Senior Tour. (His favorite trophy is a two-inch-high bowling pot, inscribed "Perfect Attendance.") Like McCord, I've never really been one for keepsakes, which is evident if you take a look around my office or library or whatever it is.

It certainly couldn't be described as a trophy room. The only trophy I really care about is a replica of the Ryder Cup, and ironically, I got that one for helping to lose the event in 1991.

There are a few other things that I would hate to lose, such as the paintings of Augusta National given to me by the Masters committee over the years, but that's pretty much it. In 20 years of hacking my way around the world, I've won two Irish Professional Championships, five European Tour events, and three tournaments in Africa.

All I have as evidence is a ghastly piece of Perspex from the BMW International in Munich, and a replica of the Scottish Open trophy, which, for some reason, has just reentered the room duct-taped to the nethermost region of Willard the Wonder Mutt. So much for the hoops game. Upon investigation, I discover that it is now a "toot catcher." Willard is not pleased, and is gnawing at his rear in an effort to free what he clearly considers to be a "toot liberator."

When I think about it, I can only say for sure that I know of the whereabouts of one of the missing pots. Never mind the trophies for the Irish Championships; I can't even remember the tournaments. I know the 1992 Madrid Open trophy is in a little hole-in-the-wall bar in Donegal Place, Belfast, called JR's. At least, that's where it was the last time I saw it. Filled with peanuts, it's serving a far more useful purpose than it would be collecting dust beside my Oxford English Dictionary, which, as regular readers of my verbicidal prose will know, serves no useful purpose, either.

As for the rest of my clangware, I have no idea where it is. The Italian Open trophy, stained with the greatest marinara sauce ever made, never made it out of Italy, and the closest thing I have to the trophy from the Open de Cannes, which I won in 1990, is in a drawer in the kitchen. It's called the Open de Bottles.

I do, however, have one of those delightful trophy jackets, from the 1989 South African PGA Championship. It's a positively electric shade of royal blue, with gold embroidery on the pocket. I wouldn't wear it to a snake-wrestling bout, but I will give it this: It's not as bad as that damned kilt-with-sleeves from Harbour Town, or worse still, Colonial.

Sporting trophies mean different things to different people, but I think the best of them have lives of their own. If you ask me, the greatest of them all is the Stanley Cup. Players on the winning team get to spend a day with it, and, more importantly, do whatever they want with it. The cup has a permanent security guard who travels with it, and as a result, it seems almost to have developed its own personality.

Despite what New Jersey Devil Sergei Brylin's baby did in it last year, the Stanley Cup was still kissed by a bunch of grown men back in May. But hey, they're hockey players.

The claret jug given to the British Open winner has had a few scrapes over the last century or so, and has more character as a result. Like some of the men who won it in its early years, it got lost for a while, and was once found in a hedge by a dog. This is a good thing.

I won the Scottish Open in 1986, and promptly lost the oldest trophy in professional golf altogether, thus adding to the mystique of the event—which is of course no longer played. This has nothing to do with me. Trust me, it'll show up somewhere, and when it does, I will look like a visionary. Then, hopefully, they will allow me back into the Gleneagles Hotel, which was the scene of the crime. Not that they were upset I lost the trophy, but they were a little miffed when I refused to pay for a magnum of '61 Margaux I had emptied into it. I'm telling you, it tasted metallic. At least, the first couple of pints did. Also, there was a dead moth in the bottle, which tasted rotten.

The Wanamaker trophy—which goes to the PGA Championship winner—as large as it is, has also been misplaced. After his win in the 1925 PGA championship, Walter Hagen, that well-known fop who was fond of the occasional adult beverage, left the bucket behind in a taxi, and it didn't reappear until someone had a garage sale some two years later.

I'm assuming the cab had a chrome interior and Wally was wearing sunglasses. I mean, the claret jug I can understand; it's a one-bottle affair. But the Wanamaker? I've read the entire sports section of *USA the Day Before Yesterday* seated on a smaller receptacle.

Hagen must have been a beauty, and the kind of man I would have loved to have hung around with. He reminds me of earlier this year at the Masters, when I bumped into Mr. Patrick Summerall, one of my greatest heroes. I said to him, "Mr. Summerall, one of my sincerest regrets is that I never got to hang out with you and Brookshire and Phil Harris, you know, back when you were on the tear." He looked at me, pointed a finger, and in that famous, minimalist, nothing-but-the-facts drone, said, "Nmmm... You wouldn't have helped."

I'm not sure about these newer trophies. You'd have to wear a welder's mask to safely look at some of the jackets, and some of the hardware is decidedly dangerous. Tom Kite won the SBC Senior event in Chicago last year, and I had to award him his prize. He looked at me and backed off like I was Edward Scissorhands. It was a piece of metal in some sort of a swooping curve, with a couple of sharp, pointy bits. Thank God Tom had that Lasik surgery, or he could have put an eye out on the damned thing.

The Trophée Lancôme is another bronze boo-boo. It's a headless, armless, legless torso with a hole through its heart. It looks like someone gave Michelangelo's David to Elmer Fudd on the opening day of wabbit season. Still, it is France, and I guess they know what they're doing.

Of all the trophies in the entire world, though, there was one that was particularly dear to me, even though I am glad to say I never won it. A few years after I turned pro, there was a group of 12 of us, friends, you know, who used to play at Royal County Down in what became known as the Open Closed Championship. The sole objective of the competitors in the event was to avoid finishing in last place, for the rules stated that whomever brought up the rear was required to display the trophy in a prominent place in his home for a period of one calendar year.

The penalty for breach of the rule was one case of Margaux, and a very expensive one at that, to be distributed among the rest of the field. The trophy was beautifully framed in a shadow box of red velvet, and would have been perfectly acceptable to the wives or girlfriends of any of us had the contents not been a pair of elderly Y-fronts.

They were not hermetically sealed, either, and through the years had developed some ghastly stains, all by themselves. You want to talk about motivation, this was something you didn't want sharing the mantelpiece with Granny's ashes.

Never in the field of human conflict have so few tried so desperately to avoid something so completely. Believe me, there was no throwing in the towel in this event. Everyone tried his utmost, right to the last hole.

It makes me wonder if every great event should have two trophies: one for the victor, and one for the guy who props up the rest of the field. If the trophy were awful enough, we might get to see the occasional battle between total losers, which, these days, could be considerably more absorbing than the duel at the top.

At which hole should you aim if you are so hung over that you see two or more of them?

— *Dan Bergthold, St. Paul, Minnesota*

If there are two, aim at the one in the middle. For more than two, just pick the closest. We are talking golf, here, Dan? Aren't we?

What's Old Is New Again

Note to self about growing old:

1. Try to be there when it's happening.
2. Try not to say stupid stuff about how much harder it was in the good old days.
3. Because it wasn't.

I may not be the most observant observer out here on the PGA Tour, but it appears to me that despite bulging purses and giant advances in equipment technology, it's as hard as ever to make a living playing golf.

Tour cards are scarcer than hen's teeth and if a pro gets one, he has to outwit, outplay, and outlast the rest while sharks that have managed to perform the task for years are circling the terrified shoal of rookie minnows. Try getting that little high-octane sphere into a small cavity in the lawn with minimal swatting with all that going on.

Of course, if you believe some of the pundits, these days golf is not the challenge it once was, and there are fewer great players to beat. Toss in all the cash and apparently the modern professional scene is a private gravy plane with one class of service. "No need to upgrade here, sir. We have window and aisle seats available, every one of them a vibrating recliner, ergonomically designed to fit your powdered buttocks exactly!"

For the record, most players on the PGA Tour still heave their own sweaty luggage around municipal airports, often accompanied by a long-suffering spouse and a couple of squelching diapers. Yummy. Okay, a courtesy car, free food, and a decent hotel room can help, but very few rookies manage to stay on Tour long enough for that kind of routine to get old.

Frankly, I'm glad I don't play for a living anymore. I mean, never mind the top few in the World Rankings. Even the guys in the lower reaches are hitting shots that, just seven years ago, I never could've contemplated. Today's courses are more difficult and less forgiving, and the holes are cut in places that would have made that groovy swinging set of the 1960s and '70s soil their sans-a-belts.

Greens have systems that suck air and water from underneath, turning what once would have been unmissable, boggy dartboards into surfaces as receptive as McCord's head while he's looking at a particularly obscure graphic from TOURCast. You should see us trying to work some of those out—we're like a herd of mules staring at a brand new gate.

No, like the advances made by athletes in other sports, golfers continue to get better, just as they always will. Yes, it's easier to hit the ball a long way and straight, but there has been no loss of talent on the PGA Tour as a result. These guys are taking advantage.

Conventional wisdom suggests that every now and then in every sport, someone like Tiger Woods or Michael Jordan or Wayne Gretzky will come along and spark a period of conventional stupidity. Back in the early 1960s, the public and even the pencil squeezers disliked Jack Nicklaus because he had the audacity to upstage Arnold Palmer. Granted, Jack usually had the decency not to upstage anyone by 15 shots. But now that Tiger is here and there is no one like Arnold around—how could there be?—everyone says, "He can't be that good, so everyone else must suck!"

Well, I disagree and I think it's an insult—to Woods and the great golfers against whom he plays—to suggest that he wins because of anything other than his otherworldly brilliance. Today's players are better than yesterday's and they're making the most of the kind of equipment that's making the game more fun for everyone. I'm not just talking about the wrenches and pellets here either; now even the clothing and accessories are state of the art.

For instance, does anyone remember what playing in the rain used to be like, before Gustbuster brollies and short-sleeve, lightweight rain jackets? Not that Tour pros spend a lot of time playing in the rain anymore. The Tour is understandably wary of personal injury suits, so if a low-pressure system starts to develop over Hawaii, chances are that, before long, instead of live golf, we're all going to be treated to a few segments of last year's final round. They will be punctuated by idiotic locker-room interviews from yours truly and the occasional light-'em-up-so-they're-good'n'-sweaty, please-God-take-me-now updates from Wadkins and Nantz.

If it's a USA Network show, you might get lucky and get a little Baywatch. Let me see: Wadkins, Nantz and me, or Pamela

Anderson running in slo-mo down the beach? You make the call.

Playing golf in bad weather, especially wind and rain, used to be a real art, and Tom Watson was the great master. He battled to victory in five Open Championships wearing a dopey-looking bucket hat, full waterproofs and that famous, insane grin. And, of course, by his side was his most vital piece of bad-weather equipment: the great Bruce Edwards.

Watson and Edwards have seen their fair share of downpours over the years, but only Edwards ever got wet. Totally selfless and seemingly four-armed, Edwards was always forging ahead and letting the master draft, safe and dry, behind the shield he created with the big red and white Ram umbrella. What a caddie! To have Edwards carry your bag is to have Ralph Lauren choose your clothes or Annie Leibovitz take your picture.

Edwards will make you look good and feel good, and no one but you will know why. It brings a lump to my throat to think of what Edwards, diagnosed with Lou Gehrig's disease, is going through, but I am comforted by the knowledge that in this, the toughest round of his life, it's still as it always was: Bruce Edwards is with Tom Watson.

Sadly, in most locker rooms, even the stench of wet golfer is a distant memory. It's hard to describe the steamy pong of damp cashmere on hot skin, combined with wet leather, decomposing grass, slow-draining urinals, Gold Bond medicated powder, cheap Clubman aftershave, buffet farts, and AquaNet. But if you left several wet yellow Labs in a chemical toilet for a couple of hours, sprinkled them with compost, then hurled them into the emergency room at your local hospital, you'd be close. Ah, the memories!

Then there's the modern golf shoe. It comes in some seriously different shapes and sizes, from instep-hugging, inflatable pumps to open-tootsied slingbacks. Some of them look like standard astronaut issue, and all of them are equipped with the worst innovation to be inflicted on the locker-room shoe-jockey since Judge Smails: the dreaded plastic cleat.

Never mind that more golfers than ever are falling on their arses. Now they're lacing up at home and avoiding the locker room altogether! A lot of Tour pros, including Tiger and Phil, frequently wear nails, but for the club golfer, the transition to Softspikes is now almost total. Personally, I miss the sound and the sparks caused by carbon steel on concrete. It's a golf noise that has almost disappeared, but there I go again, whining about the good old days, when men were men and putting lipstick on a sheep didn't make you a bad person.

Nowadays, after the rare occasion on which a player has to play in the wet, he shrugs off a lightweight, often short-sleeve, Gore-Tex shell, slips into the old loafers and slinks casually into the players lounge. Luxury, eh?

Well, maybe. But these days, any player who has managed to get there and stay there is a pretty special golfer. It's damned difficult to make money playing golf, and it always will be—whether things seem cushy or not.

My sales staff for Christmas chipped in and purchased for me the PC version of EA Sports "Tiger Woods 2004." At my age (48) and being video game challenged, I must say it is quite fun to look at the virtual remakes of those famous courses loaded into the software, even if I still cannot shoot a decent score. To my surprise the commentary provided by you and Gary McCord is very humorous and quite entertaining—it is really like you are commenting on my horrific shots. That time in the studio must have been a hoot. Have you played or listened to it yourself? Thanks for your wit and humor added to a video game.

— *John Cole, Fairfield, Ohio*

Come now, you're smoking me, right? You can't really be a sales mangler, can you? I mean you've just put two hundred words together without making a sentence. You can't possibly think McCord actually had anything to do with creating that drivel, can you? Look John, a 48-year-old man should not be playing golf video games all day. Has it occurred to you that your sales staff might be taking advantage of you? I guess it's true, when a salesman becomes ineffective in the field, they make him the "VP of Sales." I'm thinking they'll all be in a bar at this very moment, laughing their collective asses off that they got you a video game and you've forgotten completely to ask them for their numbers this week. And yes, I've played it—but not very often. I can't take the commentary.

A Moving Experience

I've moved house a few times in the last few years, and somehow I've always managed to be on the road when the actual physical stuff takes place. Until this time, that is. We've had all our stuff in storage for a couple of months and just the other day I was trapped in our new house as it was being moved in. It was quite a revelation. I was put to work by Anita, my little commandant, and had to open boxes and move furniture and all kinds of other stuff that I consider myself much too highly qualified for. However, I did discover some stuff that, because of my self-deletion from the scenes of previous moves, had been moved from attic to attic without seeing the light of day for years. I'm talking about old golf clubs here—bags and bags of them, and fossilized FootJoys, too.

In a pathetically obvious attempt to escape the torture of physical exertion, I announced that I had to go up to the club to hit a few shots with my old weapons. I fled like a dog before I got an answer, and accidentally switched my car phone off as I got in.

It might have been a pitiful excuse, but actually it turned out to be quite interesting. I started by waking up a few woodworms. I used to drive it with a gorgeous old MacGregor that was stained a beautiful honey brown with a burgundy insert. I was one of those people who clung to my woods for much longer than I should have, while everyone was shelling it 30 yards past me with metal.

In other words, my driver wasn't the only one with a wooden head. My first few swings felt a little strange in a sort of ball-not-going-anywhere kind of way, but I persevered until I caught one really flush. Which didn't go anywhere either. I tried another driver, this time one of the first I used as a pro, a laminated Jack Nicklaus Slazenger with a graphite shaft. I remembered myself as a huge knocker with this one, but now it felt like I was swinging a slinky with a loaf of bread on the end of it.

I hit all of my old clubs, and the only ones that felt any good were an old set of Phil Ritson Top-Flite irons, which were so soft that I used to be able to change the lofts by whacking them on the rubber matting outside the pro shop at Disney World. The chrome was worn off the sweetspots and the ball still melted off for the woods. I have no idea how we ever played with them. I've been as guilty as anyone about downplaying the advantage of the metalwoods, probably because when I changed up to better equipment, I thought the difference had as much to do with me. That was, until I changed down again the other day. I'd rather have stayed home and strained against the sofa. At least that's what I'm telling Anita.

I use a set of cavity-back irons and sometimes I find it difficult to shape the ball. My question is: Is it easier to shape shots using a blade iron rather than a cavity-back iron?

— *Benny Lopez, Hammond, Indiana*

Benny and the Jets: Why do you want to shape the ball? What's wrong with round?

Great Balls of Fire

Someone with way too much free time once said that at any given moment, thousands of golf balls are in the air all over the planet. Now, that's a pretty weird thought and I like it. It's like the earth is the atom, and the golf balls are the electrons or neutrons or whatever they call them, that whiz around it in orbit. Whoa, dude, like, totally cosmic.

Actually, the way things are going with the evolution of the golf ball, we're getting pretty close to making one that might make it out of the earth's atmosphere. It seems to me that with all the controversy over technological developments in the game, the lowly golf ball has escaped almost unnoticed. Everyone has been obsessed with shafts and clubheads and the only real restriction on the ball has been the 250-feet-per-second regulation. For years, manufacturers have been coming up with more and more cunning ways to try to convince us that they have finally laid the golden egg upon us.

It's been years since I actually had to buy golf balls (I, ahem, am paid good money by the people who make Stratas), but just the other day I showed up to play at a new golf course, only to discover that my bag—courtesy of some lowlife, kleptomaniac baggage handler—was a pellet-free zone. Feeling a little miffed, I strode belligerently into the pro shop, threw down my cash, and asked for a dozen of my favorite brand.

While the assistant pro was rummaging around under the counter, my eye fell upon the bewildering variety of ammunition currently available to confuse the average duffer. I had no idea. There were balls with titanium cores, some with titanium in the cover, a bunch of them with multiple covers, gel-filled ones, hard ones, soft ones, soft ones with a hard center, and hard ones with a soft center. My God, I've seen boxes of chocolates with less variety.

Nowadays, everyone seems to make a golf ball, even tire manufacturers. That means you can make a pitchmark on the green and a skidmark on the road, courtesy of the same company. Shoe manufacturers are getting in on the action, too, and, lo and behold, someone even invented a ball that McCord won a tournament with! This is the equivalent of David Copperfield making not only the elephant disappear, but the smell of the elephant as well.

Well, I don't know. This is all well and good, but it seems to me that golf balls just aren't what they used to be. Some of the spuds that were on the market when I was a lad made the game a real adventure. As I dust through the shelves of the locker in my head, images of the small ball come floating back. Of course, very few people in this country will remember that ball—1.62 inches in diameter, instead of today's 1.68—but, boy, it was a beauty to play with.

We used to have balls like the Penfold Ace, which came not only in numbers, but in spades, diamonds, clubs, and hearts. Its skin was so thin and sensitive that on the rare sunny days we had, you had to smother it in sunscreen before you hit it. Then there was the Dunlop Warwick—a substandard version of the Dunlop 65, which was a popular ball among the professionals of that time—and my personal favorite, the Spalding Dot.

When the R&A decreed back in 1990 that the 1.68-inch ball (which was always known as the "bigball"), was the only one legal for competition, it effectively knocked a lot of players clean out of the game. The small ball went farther, held its line better in the breeze, and it made the hole look bigger, too. So, in other words, some players suddenly found themselves short, crooked, and unable to putt. That normally doesn't help.

So we all had to change to the big ball, the first generation of which was quite a shock to our systems. Does anyone remember the Uniroyal Plus 6? It was so named because it was supposed to add six yards to your tee shots. It had hexagonal dimples and Uniroyal didn't mention that the six yards that it added would be in height, not distance. Of course, Uniroyal is also famous for tires, not balls.

Most manufacturers have the occasional skeleton in their closets. Anyone in R&D will tell you that sometimes you have to take a step or two backward in order to get going in the right direction again. For many years, I represented a company (which shall remain nameless) whose main area of expertise was in clubmaking, but every now and then, they'd come up with a ball they wanted their staff players to use. Most of these balls were okay, but occasionally, you'd get one that fell out of the sky like a gutshot snipe.

In order to adequately describe to you the feeling of making contact with a bad egg, I have been conducting a series of top secret tests late at night in my basement. So far the closest I've come is when I hit a Beanie Baby with a slice of freshly buttered toast. Jerry Pate actually won a U.S. Open with the ball in question, which is an indication of how wonderful a player he was. I think he probably would have won by a greater margin had he been using a pomegranate.

My problem is that I'm way too smart. I know that this is true because that's what my wife tells me, and she is never wrong. You see, I think golf ball manufacturers might have been closer to developing the perfect ball than they thought some 30 years ago—you know, when we used to get the occasional lemon that stuck to the clubface a little too long.

The self-appointed rulers of the game have decreed that the golf ball should not be permitted to travel more than 250 feet in one second, and for years the equipment companies have attempted to make a ball that will go as far as possible, and then stop as quickly as possible. This is, in my view—for want of a real word—a "golfymoron." (Come to think of it, that might be an adequate description for McCord.) We now have a generation of golf balls that leave the clubface faster than hot snot out of a chrome nostril when, in fact, the opposite would be considerably more helpful.

Just imagine if you took a swipe at the ball and it stayed glued to the clubface for about 30 seconds. You could run up to the hole and wait for it to fall off. The "compression" factor would become obsolete and would be replaced by "duration." The distance that you are able to hit the ball would now be determined by the amount of ground you're able to cover during the period the ball is stuck to the face.

So, if you're a granola muncher who works out five times a week, and can cover 300 yards in 45 seconds, then the 45-Duration ball would be for you. If, on the other hand, you are a lard-assed salad-swerver (which, incidentally, does not make you a bad person), you might want to think about the 60-Special, or alternatively a turbo-charged cart, which brings me to my second great innovation.

Sadly, I've resigned myself to riding in a cart for most of my social games. So if I have to do it, I figure I might as well make it fun. With the new "duration" ball, the longest hitters would be those with the fastest carts. Enter the NasCart.

Those namby-pamby little electric chariots with their irritating gravity brakes and loathsome governors would be replaced by growling hotrods with lumpy idling small block V-8's and side oilers. They'd pop and snarl on the downshift and spit out unburned fuel.

Given the macho nature of the average male golfer, the race to be the longest hitter would bring the added attractions of fiery pileups and loss of human life. A whole new section of the community would be drawn to the game. I already have plans for the world's first 18-hole banked oval here in Texas, where I live.

We need to shed golf's elitist image anyway, so what better way to do it than to introduce a few rednecks?

What is your opinion on Broomhandle-putters? I just read an interview where Colin Montgomerie said long putters should be banned. I know you are using one, or at one time have used one. Any ideas?

— *Pekka Loukkola, Oulu, Finland*

Pekkapickledpeppers: Let me tell you, Pekka, I miss just as many putts with the long putter as I ever did with the short one—hell, maybe more. I could have that thing bolted to one of my chins and attach it to a universal joint mounted on my not-inconsiderable stomach for additional stability and still manage to leave every putt a foot short. It's not the arrows, bubba, it's the archer. Go back to your sauna.

Captain Underpants
and the Quest for Knowledge

H o-hum. The golf season is over for us at CBS, and it's time for other sports. My head is completely full of golf knowledge at this stage, so I'm having it emptied in order to make room for football. In between, I'm tossing in a little tennis for good measure. I just got back from a weekend in New York with She-Who-Must-Be-Obeyed, and baby Erin. On Saturday, we went to Arthur Ashe Stadium to hang out with the CBS crew, and watch the action at the U.S. Open. I really wanted to see Pete Sampras vomit, but apparently that hardly ever happens. Already I was learning stuff.

As I already suspected, John McEnroe is a god. That man could start a fight in an empty room, and I think, now that I have basically retired for the year, he is the best announcer still working. I should be making the rules for golf, and he should be in charge of tennis. Bill Macatee can coordinate the clothing. If you put John and me together, it would be a no-brainer—although that's probably not the way to put it.

John misses wooden rackets, and I miss him. Tennis used to be so much more interesting when he and Nasty, and Borg, and Connors were around—or is that just me being a complete (you fill in the blank)? I enjoy the ladies' game more now, except when Richard Williams shows up. Maybe I'm just being sentimental, which would be a little unusual to say the least, but it does seem to me that technology has done a lot more to harm tennis than it has to golf.

It's everywhere though, even after the event. How about these new dope tests for athletes? Personally, I think that they could have saved themselves a lot of bother by making the ingestion of banned substances into an exhibition event for the 2000 Olympics. You know, who can do the most before their heart explodes? I miss the days of the women's discus when, you never knew, a pair of (think lower not higher) could pop out of the old leotard on the follow-through.

There's no suspense like that any more, but still, I can hardly wait for these Olympics, especially the swimming. They all have these new full-body swimsuits, made of wee swimmy molecules that make the water whoosh by quicker. How long can it be, I asked myself the other night (roughly two-thirds of the way through a bottle of Chateau Margaux), before a swimsuit finishes before the swimmer who was wearing it? I can imagine Bob Costas and the underwater camera shots of that one.

"And he's on world record pace, as he turns for the final length."

"Oh look, he's got a little rudder, Bob!"

"That's not a rudder, and his swimsuit has struck for the front!"

"I guess the water is a little on the chilly side, Bob."

It probably won't happen, and we're not going back to wood in golf, or in tennis either. Just for laughs, a little while ago, I took out one of my favorite persimmon drivers for a few holes. Bad idea, as these days I hit it short enough, and far enough sideways, with the oversize metal. Ah, progress.

Why has golf become so boring and monotonous? The "new kids on the block" simply do not have the charisma that Tiger Woods has. It has become very difficult to muster any affection for a bunch of spoiled, egotistical, and often homely millionaires. Help! I need an enthusiasm transfusion. Do you think 2004 will be bearable? Maybe if there were PGA Tour Cheerleaders... or maybe if the players had more interaction with the fans... Please God, let me love golf again!

— P.A.J., Fort Worth, Texas

It seems like I hear this lament every year. In fact, I'm pretty sure I heard or read about it when Nicklaus was challenging Palmer and Watson was taking a run at Nicklaus, when Miller was winning everything in sight, and now that Tiger's the only exciting guy around. I think there's a lot to be excited about. What about Ben Curtis's win in the United Kingdom and Shaun Micheel in the PGA Championship? I think I may have heard the spoiled and egotistical charge before as well. Homely's a first, though. The good news for the ugly guys, however, is they can usually find a much better looking wife or girlfriend than you, unless you just inherited 80 bajillion dollars. Now, Tiger's not a bad looking guy, but do you think for one minute he'd be marrying Elin if he was "popping the rag" at the airport? (That's shining shoes in case you don't know.) Funny the way that works.

PGA Tour Cheerleaders, huh? You might want to try laying off the wacky tobacky for a while, my man.

Knick and Knack

I'm one of those lucky souls who doesn't have to pay for golf stuff: you know, balls, clubs, gloves, etc. But I like to keep thunderously up to date, so the other day I visited one of those big golf stores, to see what was going on. I'm pretty unrecognizable as long as I keep my mouth shut, so I just blended in and shuffled around with the rest of the sad sacks that were there to search for something that might improve their games, and therefore, their lives.

You know, some people are really weird about this game. There was this one guy who was wandering around the store, muttering to himself, and occasionally trying something out or slipping something on. At one stage, he had a FootJoy strapped into what looked like a snow shoe on one foot, an Etonic on the other, Greg Norman's Secret on his left wrist, and a large beach ball between his knees, while he made practice swings with what looked like a baseball bat filled with water. The guy looked like Dick Van Dyke in *Mary Poppins*.

I felt like handing him a harmonica and ramming a trumpet up his butt, but then I remembered I was in Texas, so I decided against it. He probably had a master's degree in quantum mechanics, and he might have been carrying a concealed nuclear warhead.

Maybe it was just me, but it seemed there was a lot of bizarre stuff for sale—you know, the kind of things that only a certifiable raving golf nutcase would buy. And I thought to myself, surely there couldn't be that many of those around, could there? But in a departure from my normal M.O., and against all my better instincts, I decided to do some research. So I pulled aside one of the sales associates, a pimply youth, and revealed my identity.

He didn't know who I was, even after I had told him. But, in defense of my own undeniable famousness, it appeared that he didn't know who he was either, so I let all the air out of him, and went to find somebody else. I needed to find the kind of sick, Golf Channel–watching, psychopathic shank victim who should be working in such an establishment. It didn't take long before I had cornered "Norm," who was over in men's apparel, wearing a pair of those guaranteed-never-to-get-you-laid plus-twos, fog-lamp glasses, and an overdose-of-Zoloft grin.

Norm had a spectacular speech impediment, to which he seemed quite oblivious, but he turned out to be a veritable unused mineshaft of obscure information. Almost drowning me in sputum, he ran through the store's top sellers at breakneck speed and with frightening accuracy.

I must admit, I was quite taken aback at both the volume of the saliva Norm was capable of producing and the amount of totally useless crap that he was peddling to the unsuspecting general public. I couldn't fathom that there were people in this country who were gullible enough to believe that any of this stuff might make them into a better golfer!

I thought, What sort of an idiot would spend a fortune on something so obviously full of hot air, or believe such exaggerated claims? Then I remembered that CBS hired me and that *Golf*

*M*agazine actually gives me money to write this majestic piece of sports journalism, which is ribbed and guaranteed to increase your reading pleasure or they will give you my money back.

It's at times like these that I wish this print were much smaller. But anyway, perhaps there's something to this. Maybe, if you strap on the patented "Elbow and Love-Handle Truss," and hit 10 large buckets of "Correct-O-Nuts" with a laser beam on the bill of your weighted "Head-Down Helmet," tomorrow, when you take it all off, you might shoot lower. I mean if you think about it (which you shouldn't), you should! The game would have to be a little easier if you weren't wearing all that crap, wouldn't it?

That's it! What a stroke of genius, and how fitting, that in golf, which is an impossible sport, scientists could create such a simple way to help improve the average Joe. I can see the applications in other sports already. In swimming, for instance, how long can it be before we see the introduction of the new, stainless steel, full-body Speedo?

I can see the infomercial for it now: Mark Spitz, encased in the new training aid, drowning at the bottom of the pool, followed by that Irish girl—you know, the one that swam like an anchor the year before, but the next thing you knew she'd won 17 gold medals? She developed gills and had a dorsal buttock, but she didn't do any drugs.

"After just one session in the new 'Steelo,' we guarantee you (if you're not dead) that afterward, you will find swimming a lot easier!"

Yeah, I imagine so. And if you are dead, you can have your money back. I ordered one of those golf-training aids (which shall remain both nameless and useless) a while ago and sent it straight back, just to see if they would actually send me a refund. It promised, "Six to eight shots off my scores, or my money back!"

"Dadgummit!" I thought. "If this puppy works, I'm hangin' up the microphone and headin' back out there, to whup me a whole can of Tiger ass!"

Turns out, they had me on a technicality because I never used it. They sent it back. Perfect, I thought. Just what I need, a band for my left wrist, attached by rubber surgical tubing to an alligator scrotum clip, to stop me from "over-swinging." No kidding, I guess it would, but I'm in no mood to find out, and they can keep their lousy $19.95. How the hell did they know it hadn't been used? That's what I want to know. Not that it matters, as I'd probably need more than eight shots of a start to get in front of you-know-who.

The truth is, none of this upsets me nearly as much as the whole knick-knack industry, which was also heavily represented in this store. I mean, I'm in a golf discount warehouse, and they're selling wall-mounted, rubberized, singing fish. Now, that's Wal-Mart territory, where at least you can buy a shotgun as well, so that you can line up the fish with that hideous dancing Santa and blow the damn things to bits.

I believe that there is no place for knickknacks in this modern world of ours. The words themselves are obnoxious enough. Knick and Knack. They sound like a pair of irritating, fuzzy, TV rodents, and I don't know about any of you, but I want a Teletubby piñata party for my 43rd birthday. But I digress.

Golf knick-knacks are utterly horrifying, and it's the people who have to make them that I feel sorry for. Imagine spending your working hours in a glass-blowing sweatshop, making kelly green copies of tiny, sharp-nosed, pipe-smoking figures breaking nasty little golf clubs over their knobby little knees, titled "The Angry Leprechaun Ashtray."

"Lord, rather let me fling myself under the sacred wheels of your electric golf cart, as you make the celestial turn in 29 and burn holy rubber from the great halfway house in the sky. Much more acceptable would it be to writhe like road kill, stained with the angelic mustard from your heavenly wiener, and spend eternity having divots taken from my unworthy personage by the bounceless sole of your 60-degree wedge, than to have to make one of those accursed ashtrays."

If you haven't caught the drift that I don't like these things by now, you are officially not paying attention. Spare a thought also for the person sitting in the woodshop, stenciling on a picture frame—underneath a print of a bunch of tweed-infested old duffers—those words we know so well: "Old golfers never die." Yes, we know they never die, and we are also very well aware of what they lose.

I just hope that 150 years from now, "The Antiques Roadshow" is still on the air, and that some kind, gray-haired old lady brings in that very same print. There will be a nerdy looking guy, with dandruff and a pocket square, who will listen patiently as the old lady explains how it has been in her family for five generations, and to be honest, she has absolutely no idea of its value, although she did have a great uncle Norm, who told her mother once that it was one of a kind and very valuable. Then, the nerdy guy will smile, pick up the print, and smash it over the old lady's head, and in a fit of foaming-at-the-mouth insanity, tell her that 150 years ago, it was a worthless piece of crap, which is precisely the estimate he would be inclined to give her now.

Then, in my ideal future world, on the floor, among the fragments of her precious family heirloom, the old lady would find a hand-written letter from Bobby Jones to Ben Hogan, in which Mr. Jones had revealed the secret of golf.

Hey, I like old ladies, okay?

I'm a 3-handicap. I have one problem of sliding my hips through the downswing instead of turning. Any drills to help me improve? Thanks.

— *Trace Dandrea, Boise, Idaho*

Trace: Is that a guy's name? Fly to Nashville, Tennessee. Rent a van. Drive to the Jack Daniels Distillery in Lynchburg. Buy a barrel of their finest bourbon. (Don't get caught drinking any in Lynchburg, though; believe it or not, it's a dry county). Drive all the way back to Boise. Invite all your friends over for a party. Drink the barrel dry. After it's empty, and the cops and the firemen have all left, take the top off the barrel. Go out back, climb in the barrel and start swinging, my man. Problemo solvedo!

Information Overload

I feel kind of sorry for the average golfer these days. Thirty years ago, kitting yourself out with a good set of clubs, nice shoes, a glove, and a dozen decent balls was a fairly simple affair. But these days, with the amount of quality equipment on the market, it's an expensive mind-bender. Of course, it's never been a problem for the Tour pro, who gets all the best stuff flung at him by the reps on the range. He usually takes a whack with a bunch of clubs, hums and hahs a little, and then takes armfuls of them home to his pals under the pretense of a little "home testing." Yeah, right. What happens is a few more average golfers are equipped with tools entirely unsuitable for their standard of handiwork.

So, how should the amateur swordsman choose his weapons? Probably not as follows, but in golf, no matter at what level we play, we all have delusions.

People are always sending me books, most of which are collecting dust on the shelves of my study. The other day, however, one arrived that piqued my interest. In the pile of flyers, bills, and ladies' undergarment catalogs heaped on the hall floor lay a small, plain, green-covered paperback with the title, *The Darrell Survey 2002 Golf Equipment Almanac.*

Following a close but thorough examination of Push-Up & Thong Weekly, I settled down in the old La-Z-Boy to see if there was anything I didn't already know in the pages of what is being touted as golf's version of the auto trade's Blue Book. I wanted to find out juicy tidbits like the trade-in value of my old Wilson shag bag or my mint-condition Uniroyal Plus 6 hexagonal dimple-ball with the elastic hanging out.

Alas, no luck on anything like that, but as it happens, there is a lot of stuff in there I didn't know, even more stuff I don't want to know, and a complete absence of certain vital information that people like me would find invaluable when trying to make an informed choice about tackle.

For instance, did you know that about 52 percent of all golfers over the age of 50 wear FootJoy golf shoes? Damned if I did, but my question would be this: Of that 52 percent, how many of them wear those FootJoys to drive home slowly in the fast lane with their left-turn signal blinking all the way? They need to research that and get back to me.

I'd like to know a bunch of other things about golf-shoe performance, too. Like, which is the best alternative spike to wear on the beer-drenched tiled floor of a cheesy topless bar? Never mind your sidehill lies, pal; you need to keep your head up when you cross the blue line in a place like that. Another thing: Why hasn't anyone designed a golf shoe with a little speaker in the toe that can simulate the sound of metal spikes on concrete? I miss that.

And after a three-putt, why do you never see anyone arc-welding themselves to a cart path in a fit of tap-dancing fury on their way to the next tee anymore? It was one of the most spectacular sights in golf, but sadly, with the dawn of Softspikes, it's probably gone forever. Now people just melt rubber and spend the rest of the day smelling like an electrical fire.

Flicking backward (as is my wont) through the book, I came upon page after page of sideways bar charts on interesting stuff like the overall satisfaction rating on putter brands by age, handicap, and feature (whatever that means). But time after time I was puzzled by the absence of data on the truly important issues, such as putter durability.

The Ping Anser 2 is a favorite among all handicaps and ages, but why that is so is not revealed. Personally, I think it's because you can beat the crap out of, dig up, and mulch a medium-sized conifer with a Ping Anser 2, and afterward, you still have something to putt with.

One of my favorite sections of the book is the bit where they show the total and average amount of money per tournament won by each piece of equipment used on the PGA Tour. It's sort of an equipment order of merit, or money-list thingy. The whole concept is brilliantly flawed in that it doesn't mention the amount of money the players are paid to play the aforementioned equipment. To me, that would be the real stat. Then we could compare the average amount of money per start that the Nike ball wins to the amount Phil Knight pays Tiger to play, it divided by the amount of tournaments Tiger plays. I'm guessing, but I think we're talking about a loss leader there. (Ha! Who'd have thought we could ever legitimately call Tiger a loss leader? This book could be brilliant with a little creative editing.)

How about the golfer who wants the entire package: as in the best shoes, shirt, shafts, grips, irons, wedges, glove, ball, driver, fairway woods, putter, and golf bag? With *The Darrell Survey 2002 Golf Equipment Almanac*, access to NASA's mainframe, and the help of the entire workforce at IBM for a couple of months, why, it should be a dawdle to figure out what to wear and play.

By combining the "shirt brands by handicap" figures with the "shirt brands by age" info and factoring in your age and handicap, it's relatively easy to figure out that if you happen to be a 44-year-old with a handicap in the 11 to 20 range, you should be wearing a one-sleeved, Cutter & Ashpolo, size extra-medium—presumably with matching tighty-whities.

This little book is a lot of fun, but like I said, there are a number of glaring oversights and omissions. One of the most worrisome is the lack of data on the margin of error, which as we all know, exists in every poll, no matter how meticulously it is taken.

I remember the Darrell Surveyors (or, "Bagspies," as they were known) from my playing days. Sneaking furtively around the practice ground with clipboards and leopard-crawling under the ropes onto the first tee, they were occasionally intercepted by the alert caddie or even a player who might just have had a vested interest in concealing the true identity of what lay beneath his head covers or in his ball pocket. The dirty dogs. Oh, yes, sometimes a player can be paid a lot of money to swing a set of clubs, and money is "corruption," except most of the letters in it are different. Stay with me here, I'm on to something.

You see, I know from first-hand experience that there is jiggery-pokery going on. I remember playing with a guy who was 20 yards behind me off the tee one day and 30 yards in front the next. (Well, I only vaguely remember, because I was a little hung over the morning of the second round, and we had a really early tee time, but you know what I mean.) Believe me, if a guy is whistling on the first tee, with his hands buried deep in his pockets and his head turned to one side, there is almost certainly some kind of ball-tampering going on. Call me a genius, or a paranoid freak with a conspiracy theory, but do you really think McCord is playing with a limp Noodle?

All right, maybe that's not such a good example, but who says the Darrell arms inspectors have been given full access to the suspected sites, and even if they have, are they qualified enough to tell whether or not the coefficient of any given driver has been sufficiently restitutionalized? Ask yourself that! Do you think that you could tell the difference between a set of blank Mizuno forgings and a set of leaded-up Wilson FG17s? Exactly! You thought the Wilson FG17 was a fighter plane, didn't you?

Don't worry, it doesn't make you a bad person, and here's what I think: *The Darrell Survey 2002 Golf Equipment Almanac* is an essential piece of literature for the golfer who has everything and is having a hell of a time trying to figure out what goes with which, into where, and why. It's about time we had a manual to follow here, and other sports could take a leaf or two out of this book.

For instance, my most recently discovered passion is fly-fishing, and I had a hell of a time getting myself equipment that would make me an expert overnight. No *Darrell Survey* available there, so I had to rely on my own instinct, which has a few gaps in it, and, as a consequence, I was hoodwinked by a slick salesman. It's the old story: Get the customer on the line and then play him like a sick mullet. It was obvious I needed the inflatable trout decoys, but only after a very unsuccessful afternoon spent up to my nads in freezing cold water did it become apparent that the buggers needed their little anchors, which are, of course, sold separately.

Talk about an investment going down the Suwanee. But with *The Darrell Survey 2002 Golf Equipment Almanac*, golfers everywhere can have that reassuring feeling that the purchase they make will be the right one, at least until your shirt starts a nipple-rash after its first wash and your long irons, like all long irons, are unhittable. Still, you'll know which 7-, 9-, and 11- woods to buy instead.

Summer

Naked Came the Dangler

I've suspected it for decades, but now it's official. The end of the world is upon us. The legendary Portmarnock Golf Club in Dublin, home of the Irish Open and probably the best course in Ireland, has been sued for discrimination against females, and found guilty. Will the club be fined or closed? Oh no, dear readers, this is much more bloody serious. Believe it or not, a judge (a *chick* judge) has ordered that the clubhouse bar be closed for one week.

A whole week! Let me remind you, this is Ireland we're talking about, not Utah. I could understand a symbolic minute of abstinence, but a whole week of dryness at an Irish golf club? It could cause another civil war.

I might have been in this legal wrangle myself, as a Portmarnock member, if not for an unfortunate misunderstanding in the locker room at the Irish Open in 1986, when I was accused by the then-oldest member of actually *being* a woman. The myopic old fart had a conniption when he saw me mincing toward him, love-handles akimbo. "Young lady!" he screamed. "Put your drawers on immediately!"

That was the last time I failed to follow the unwritten men's-locker-room code, which, should it ever show up in print (perish the thought), would go something like this:

A gentleman member should never appear naked until such time as he has rendered himself— by warm soaping or other privately conceived means—recognizable as a male of the species.

I suppose it's acceptable to wander around the locker room, boys-out, but I find it a little weird. Do the ladies act that way over on their side of the clubhouse? Dear God, I hope I never find out.

But back to the judge's ruling, a heinous act that strikes at the very heart of the nation. In all seriousness, I believe that all-male clubs provide an essential service. To women. The point is this: Elderly white men cherish every opportunity to mill around naked, farting bitter little clouds of cheap talcum powder and leaving half-squeezed tubes of Vitalis in the sinks, even though most of their hair grows from the neck down. But their wives won't allow it. She-Who-Must-Be-Obeyed certainly won't have such behavior in her house and does not want to hear locker-room talk, which usually centers on market fluctuations or how the latest blonde Fox News anchor is *brilliant* compared to that Canadian pinko Peter Jennings.

And so we men have no choice: We must gather naked at golf clubs.

Still, since the Portmarnock incident these sad little men-only sanctums have been emotional minefields to me. I can barely stand to see *myself* naked. The other day I was standing fully clothed by a washbasin when I was joined by a horribly sprightly 87-year-old nudist who took up a wide stance at the sink next to me and began to hum while brushing his teeth. (I know you're not supposed to look, but he took his teeth *out* to do it.) It was then that I let down my guard and looked lower, and noted that gravity is a cruel master indeed. Leafing through the naked-elderly-person-at-next-washtub protocol manual in my mind, I found no entry under *Avoiding Octogenarian Pendulum.* Then I realized that its owner had put his teeth back in and was looking at me.

"What are you staring at, sonny?"

It was hard to say, really. It was like two Titleists on a string hanging from a mushroom in a chickadee nest. And there I was, busted in a bathroom, way too interested in another man's wobblies.

I apologized and beat a hasty retreat to my rental car, where I turned on the AC and the radio, assumed a fetal position and sucked my thumb for the first time since my 19th birthday. The next song up was the Village People's "YMCA," and I haven't been the same since.

I'm no barrister, but I have a solution to the Portmarnock problem. Let the women in, I say. Let them gaze upon the cottage cheese of our inner thighs, sit upon our cold, wet porcelain and wander around naked. Whereupon Judge Mary Collins can have mercy and reopen the bar. Because you know the photos will make the Internet, and then we'll all need a stiff drink.

As I watched the third round of the Masters, I couldn't help but notice the gallery. Is it just the camera shots I saw, or were there really almost no African Americans in the gallery at Augusta? Side note: My name for Hootie and his cohorts: Hootie and the Blowhards (yep—instead of "Hootie and the Blowfish"). I absolutely LOVE your column—your quick wit leaves me breathless with laughter. Your insights on the game and its denizens are priceless. Thank you!

— *Theresa Turner*

Don't be watching the mail for that membership application to Augusta anytime soon, hon.

All Things Being Equal

B oy, do we live in strange times. The most popular shows on television are shallow pantomimes—based on lies, avarice, and deception—that rely on perhaps the oldest form of human entertainment: the public humiliation of a previously exalted individual. We don't lock people in the stocks and throw vegetables at them anymore; we toss them off the island or give the rose to someone else, but it's pretty much the same thing. Ha, ha, ha, you lose.

At the time of this writing, I don't know the outcome of *Survivor*'s battle of the sexes, but it doesn't really matter, as we have our own little reality show going on in golf. Suzy does Hartford, Annika saddles up in Fort Worth, and now, as if to accelerate the demise of civilization as we know it, Brian Kontak wants to play in the U.S. Women's Open.

Okay, I know I'm not the ref in this one, but I'm calling a TV timeout anyway. I need to get a couple of things straight here before I can move on with my miserable male existence.

What the hell is Brian thinking? Regulations for both the LPGA and the USGA women's events state that in order to qualify, a competitor must be born a female, which means that McCord might still have a shot. But the rest of us are screwed.

Surely the bottom line is simple common sense. Yes, Annika is taking away a spot from a veteran, or a rookie, or whomever, but this would only be a bad thing if the Bank of America Colonial were being run for the sole benefit of the Tour pros. I think this is hardly the case. Bank of America is doing this gig for the good of the company and its shareholders, so the addition of the best female player on the planet and all the publicity she brings with her is ultimately a very good thing for them.

These days title sponsors are hard enough to come by, and we need to take better care of those willing to commit this kind of money. Provided we can act like the gentlemen we're supposed to be and show these two courageous ladies the respect they deserve, this situation will benefit everyone involved. But if even one of us throws a Miss Piggy fit and demands to be allowed to play with the girls, he runs the risk of making the rest of us look like a pack of wussies.

This is not rocket science. Retaliation is only justifiable if there is something to be gained. Think of it in children's hockey terms and you'll get the idea. Two groups of children are playing ice hockey—girls at one end of the pond and boys at the other. The girl goalie clears the puck, and the best girl skates into the middle of the boys to retrieve it.

One of the boys decides to have a little fun and knocks her roughly to the ice, upon which she gets up, forces her way through a forest of sticks, recovers the puck, skates around a couple of defensemen, scores on a backhand shot, and, pausing only to knock three teeth out of the fat kid who checked her, glides back to the girlie end.

Whoa, Nellie! There are a couple of ways to handle this. The boys can either do what boys do, which is form a pact among blood brothers to cover up the debacle and agree to deny that any of them was there when this never happened, or toss fatty off the team and ask puck-girl to join them.

The only truly fatal mistake would be for one of the boys to barge into the girls' game. Sure, he could look skillful and strong. Yes, he'd get more of the puck, and he'd score more goals, and no, none of the girls would think he was a hero. Or smart. They'd think he was a bully, a cheat, and a moron.

"So, you beat the girls? Well done, you giant of a man!" (Not.)

And now for Suzy, whose story I think is even better than Annika's. The thing about Suzy Whaley that's been glossed over is that she is a member of the greatest association in professional sport, the PGA of America. A PGA professional has to be a lot of things: manager, mentor, merchandizer, coach, player, and sometimes—yes, I'm sorry to break the news—even a woman. Suzy won the right to play in the Greater Hartford Open by winning the Connecticut PGA Section, which until her historic victory had yielded only hairy champions.

And yes, she played from different tees, and at this point (for the benefit of those who seem to have a low threshold of understanding), let me reemphasize that Suzy Whaley is a WOMAN! Suzy Whaley isn't taking this spot away from anyone; she won it, fair and square.

The story here is one of two ladies with enough self-esteem to take a chance, step up, and test themselves at a higher level, at which the opposition has an unfair advantage. And of one man who for some reason is convinced it'd be good idea to take a step down and see how he can do at a lower level where he clearly has an unfair advantage. In an attempt to imagine a positive outcome for Brian, I've arranged all nine of my brain cells into every possible configuration, and as far as I can tell, there are only two possibilities, neither of which is attractive. I'm going with the second one first.

B. Brian loses to a woman, or women.

A. Brian wins the U.S. Women's Open and cries at the prize giving.

Okay, I just thought of another:

F. Brian gets kidnapped by a posse of militant LPGA players who wax his entire body, smother him in Old Spice aftershave, and toss him naked into the offices of *Maxim* magazine. (This wouldn't be good, either.)

We simply have to stop Brian, even if it means a calculated intervention. I mean, it's not like this is a cut-and-dried situation where some poor sap has been locked up alone for days in a rubber room with nothing else in it but a giant, red button that reads "DO NOT PUSH."

There should be dozens of flashing neon signs between Brian and his desire to wind up in a situation where he would hit a tee shot miles past his closest competitor—signs like "MAKE YOUR NEXT LEGAL U-TURN" and "STOP SMOKING THAT STUFF!" I imagine one of the first I'd notice would be "YOU WANT TO DO F&@*ING WHAT?"

Of course, we all just know there has to be some attorney working pro-bonehead in the middle of this one. Or maybe it's the television exec who dreamed up the concept for "America's Stupidest People," or "American Idol," as some people call it.

As I said earlier, these days there's nothing more entertaining than astonishingly stupid people who are willing to make spectacles of themselves. The performers in these sad shows are obviously people who don't have anyone around who cares about them enough to tell them they're making enormous errors of judgment.

For what it's worth, I'm there for Brian, whom I suspect underneath it all is just a confused guy like me. Brian, unless you want every female at the table to stand when you get up to go to the squirtatorium, and for one of them to hold the door for you on the way out, please, for the love of Tim Herron in a tutu, stick to playing with the guys. I don't think it's possible (or for that matter even healthy), to have what some call equality across the board. And while I doubt we'll ever be regarded as the fairer sex, I think we should probably try to be fair when it really matters.

Mind you, it might be hilarious to watch. Okay, pal, on second thought, go right ahead. Make America happy!

David, is there any substance to the rumor that Tiger's contract with the PGA requires that no one but he can wear a predominantly red shirt during the final round of a major? Unless, of course, he has missed the cut, which we all know won't happen before 2025 at the earliest.

— *Mike Guillory, Oberlin, Louisiana*

Where does this crap get started? In the first place, Tiger doesn't have a contract with the PGA Tour. He's a member of the Tour and shows on the weeks he wants to play and wears whatever the hell he wants. The players have a rule book they put out every year and nowhere in there does it make any reference to what color apparel anyone wears. They have references to the type of things they may wear, such as no shorts, but not the color. If they didn't, Jesper Parnevik would show up in stuff you really couldn't bear to look at! Now, if Nike wanted to tell their players what color they could wear on Sunday, that's up to them, but the Tour has nothing to do with that.

In the Olympic Spirit

AMERICAN AIRLINES FLIGHT 1427, SOMEWHERE OVER EASTERN NEW MEXICO (February 23) — These days, I tend to watch most televised sporting events in a series of leisurely spaced casual glances. But I have to admit, since I got home from the West Coast Swing, I've been riveted to the Winter Olympics. So much so that as I write, I'm heading to Winter Park, Colorado, with my sons with every intention of falling head-first down a mountain. The school ski-trip needed a chaperone or two and apparently I'm qualified to look after someone else's teenagers. Oh yeah. The fact that I'm the man their parents warned them about is irrelevant. We're supposed to be staying at the Y, but I don't think I can do that. No room service, thin toilet paper, communal TV room, and no bar.

Wait a minute... no bar? Did I really say that?

I did and it has just struck me that it might be true. Other people's children and no bar. That does it for me: one of those things isn't going to happen. The minute I get there, I'm finding the nearest Four Seasons, and getting a ground floor room that I can ski out of. That way, I can leave the sliding door open and use the sofa as an airbag when I ski back in. I've mastered every part of this sport except the stopping bit, which is awkward at times, and something I prefer to do in the privacy of my own room.

I was watching the Olympics last night and I have to say I felt a little sorry for the figure skaters. I love watching skating, with all its giggling, squealing, tears, tight buttocks, and sequins. And that's just the men. The ladies are even more fun, especially when someone like Sarah Hughes shows up. She reminded me of Tiger Woods in so many ways. Except of course she's white and a girl.

But when Tiger first appeared he displayed the same mannerisms, had the same unconscious smile, and played golf the way Hughes skated last night—with blissed-out, it's-incredible-to-be-here abandon. Golf needed Tiger, and boy, does skating need Sarah Hughes. In fact, Sarah probably isn't enough to save skating, or the Winter Olympics for that matter. It's time for the IOC to get honest about this. I mean, if the judges are getting paid, I think we might as well pay the athletes, too.

Oh yeah, I forgot. They are getting paid.

Now that I come to think of it, the rules of some of these winter pastimes probably should be blended with other sports. For instance, the figure skating pairs could use a little help from ice hockey. There should be fighting for a start. Bitch-slapping on ice would be brilliant to watch. Hell, we had cross-checking in the warm-ups this year, so why not go the whole hog?

Then there's the bobsled. Oh man, I love the bobsled, but I would love to see a little NASCAR action thrown in. Make the run four times as wide, and make them qualify for the pole position. Drafting, swappin' paint, and sleds spinning out and hitting the wall because of Red Man loogies on the ice. YEEEEHAAW!

Here's a good one for you. Instead of the two-man luge between consenting adults, how about we have two big naked fat guys in an inner tube?

Hmm... maybe you're right. How would they stop? I can see it now, six hundred pounds of quivering, naked skin and black rubber, covered with Sheetrock and splinters in the middle of the Mormon Tabernacle. Play that funky music, white boy. Wait a minute, we're landing here. This'll have to be continued elsewhere.

Later that day, in a heavily disguised Motel 6, which is buried in gray snow. Stopped halfway up the hill to buy fresh habanero beef jerky, most of which was consumed by youngest son...

Now the Russians and the South Koreans are talking about pulling out. Somebody needs to suck it up, get their chin off the ice, loosen the drawstring on their codpiece, or whatever. Although much of this could have been avoided if someone at the IOC had had the brains to invite the 1980 Russian hockey team to join the Americans in the lighting of the flame. The worst that could have happened was a massive fight for the torch might've broken out between a bunch of toothless old guys, which would've been great TV anyway. In these strange days, the recognition that the Russians were part of that magic moment might have gone a long way. We were enemies then, but aren't we friends now?

Like I said, I feel sorry for the figure skaters. How does anyone who ever won a medal know if somebody wasn't leaned on? The only thing lacking from the coverage of figure skating was Conan O'Brien's famous guest interviewer at the Westminster Dog Show: Triumph, the insult dog.

In fact, I think the figure skating judges and the Westminster judges might be the same people. I've never seen them together.

"And now, the winners of the gold medal... for me to poop on!"

Maybe I was busy or something but I totally missed the R&A adopting the USGA ball size. Was the smaller ball better in windy conditions? And with tournament golf bags being bigger than my Aunt Wanda, how many clubs does a professional travel with? What other stuff is in the bag? Thanks for all the laughs. I have reoccurring nightmares of McCord in a rubber teddy. Please suggest a cure.

— *Harry Heilmann, Silver Plume, Colorado*

The small ball was longer and easier to hit into the wind and crosswind, but it was tougher to fidget with around the green. Personally, I thought the British changed because the bigger ball was more difficult for English Setters to swallow and they were eating them by the gross. They proved to be difficult to, um, let's say, pass. Vets all over the place had to go in and do something like a Dunlop Cesarean section.

Pros play with 14 clubs in accordance with the rules. They don't travel with many more, although they may have an extra putter, wedge, or driver if they're experimenting with something. All of the club manufacturers dispatch a mobile club repair facility to virtually every tournament in the country, so if the pro needs something repaired or replaced or wants to try something new, they are right there to accommodate them. The caddie is hauling around 40 to 50 pounds every day as it is, so they don't take a lot of extra stuff. Generally they have the same stuff you carry around in yours: extra gloves, balls, Preparation H, tees, ball markers, narcotics, and whiskey.

The only cure for recurring dreams of McCord in a rubber teddy is to imagine him without the teddy and standing in front of you with nothing on but a red silk, high-cut thong bikini with the "Magnum Pouch." I guarantee you will wake up screaming every time, but you *will* wake up.

those who like to dress up and play, "Let's Make the Rules," routinely seem to find worthless the opinions of men such as these? (That was majestically pompous, I feel.)

Jack suggested a few years ago that the ball *continued on page 170*

Rules of Engagement

Well, hi-de-ho and fiddle-de-dee, here we go again. Another controversy about equipment and who gets to make the Rules. Now I'm reading that some people believe there should be two sets of Rules, one for amateurs and one for professionals.

Here's news that's actually not just in: That's the way it's been for years. Every organization of tour professionals in the world has its own set of local rules, or modifications, which are designed to allow for the fact that these people have to make a living by playing golf.

Some of them, such as Arnold Palmer and Jack Nicklaus, are people I would consider to be experts in their field... you know, at the cutting edge, maybe? They both know that the game has changed since their glory days and that it's now possible, with all this modern equipment, to hit shots they never would have dreamed of hitting.

So, a person might ask, why is it that those who like to dress up and play "Let's Make the Rules" routinely seem to find worthless the opinions of men such as these? (That was majestically pompous, I feel.)

Jack suggested a few years ago that the ball should be slowed down, but the experts disagreed, right around the same time they figured out that the square groove lawsuit wasn't such a brilliant idea after all. The fact that Tour players were reluctant to use square grooves should have been a dead giveaway, but there were a bunch of attorneys who would have felt left out if anyone had noticed that.

If anyone who mattered had taken Jack's advice, and the ball wasn't going so far today, a lot of the money currently being wasted on legal fees could be used for teaching underprivileged kids how to smoke a driver down the middle instead of a crack pipe down the alley, and the trampoline effect would still be a twisted ankle.

Instead, we have a fight between one organization with too much money and another with not enough sense. If we're not careful here, this is going to turn into boxing. If this were a heavyweight bout (and it would appear that it is), as usual, the enemy appears to be in the process of purchasing the advertising space on the soles of the USGA's feet.

The game is changing, just as it always has, but the strange thing is, nothing much is new. Metalwoods were invented more than a century ago, even ones with bouncy faces. I recall the XL adjustable spring-face driver by George F. Wilford, the introduction of which inspired a writer in the December 1895 issue of *Golf* to predict that it was only a matter of time before some idiot showed up with a dynamite cartridge in the face of his driver.

None of this nonsense would be necessary if all who played the game followed Uncle Dickie's philosophy. Because the original Rules of Golf required that the ball be played from where it lay, golf club manufacturers were forced to come up with a club to fit every occasion. Uncle Dickie has the finest collection of these clubs in the world, and boy, the game must have been fun when they were used. Wouldn't you like to see Tiger playing out of a couple of inches of casual water with an iron designed specifically for the task? Or how about the sight of the elegant Steve Elkington clipping one delicately off the top of a cow turd with one of Hamish McShug's patented splatterguard niblicks?

Hey, golf could have died out a long time ago like other sports that didn't catch on, such as catching the javelin and heading the shot. Change is good. Without it, we'd probably still be wearing three-piece Harris Tweed suits or appalling tartans, and trying to whack a badger's testicle stuffed with gannet feathers out of sandy hollows that were formed by rutting sheep. Although now that I come to think of it, that does sound rather intriguing, in a Deion-Sanders-meets-Old-Tom-Morris sort of way. But I digress.

The point is, very few people throw the discus these days, and it's probably because there are plenty of Frisbees around. That's progress for you, and the reality of our situation is that about 95 percent of the people who play golf pay absolutely no attention to the Rules anyway, which is fine as long as they are having fun.

Obviously, maintaining the integrity of this game at the serious amateur level is important. I have no problem with that, but in the words of the apparently immortal Keith Richards, "There's a difference between scratching your backside and tearing yourself a new one." Thankfully, there just aren't that many serious amateurs around. I mean, I don't know about you, but I think serious professionals are bad enough.

Even though I'm a pro, and always will be, I play in the real golf world now, where the game seems to be more fun than it used to be. Most of the people I play with are just like me (except they totally suck at golf). I'm talking about cold beers and mustard stains. Fat guys in bad shorts who will deliberately store intestinal gas for the express purpose of freaking out serious amateurs at the top of their backswings. Strategic intercontinental ballistic belchers that couldn't get down to single digits if they cut off a thumb and eight fingers. My people! I love these guys, for whom trash-talking is a sign of affection, and playing a game is still about acting like a child.

The bottom line is this: The current governing bodies have no chance of winning a fight against anyone who makes anything that has even an outside chance of making this game more fun to play. Anyone who takes golf too seriously should turn pro and they'll find out soon enough that the Rules are different.

This is not about giving the USGA or the R&A a hard time. They make the Rules for the amateur game, run their championships, and do an outstanding job of it. If, however, we have equipment that needs to be tested, it should be tested by people who, in the heat of battle, know what it is capable of doing. This is why the U.S. Air Force relies on the opinions of everyone between, say, a 24-year-old with lightning reactions, like Tiger Woods, and a 70-ish legend who has seen it all, like Arnold Palmer. Or Chuck Yeager.

Lives may not depend on golf's Rules of engagement, but livelihoods sometimes do. It's time for the pro Tours to get together and at least end this nonsense for those who feed a family by trying to get a small piece of plastic into a hole in the ground by beating it with a stick. Ultimately, golf will always be its own watchdog and this is like listening to an argument between two fleas, both of which think they own the damn thing. It's just a dog. It will scratch wherever it itches, and I think it's probably too late to do anything about this one's balls. Anyway, we need it to breed.

If you arm even a low handicap golfer with a weapon that promises an extra ten yards, he will spend most of his time 10 yards deeper in the woods. The point is, he won't care. But off one of his rare straight ones, he might hit the par-5 sixth with a 4-iron, and that is something he will care about. It will widen his eyes, make his tale taller, and make him feel so good that he might want to share the feeling with his kids.

I vividly remember the feeling I had the first time I got a ball in the air with a wooden club. It was a cut-down, brown-shafted, shiny, leather-gripped, old sheep-beater of a 2-wood, with the whipping unraveled halfway up the shaft, and the ball was yellowing and spewing elastic. I was 34 years old and playing in the German Open.

Okay, I was nine, and I had snuck onto the practice ground at dusk. I remember feeling the sweetness and then seeing the ball briefly: a little black dot, silhouetted against a sky all streaked with silver and pink, hanging over black chimneys and rooftops. And then it was gone. The hair stood up on the back of my neck, and the goose bumps flooded me so fast, I shuddered. That was almost 35 years ago, and I've been fascinated ever since.

This is still an impossibly difficult game, and anything that makes it more enjoyable or easier to pick up is just fine by me.

Do you think that "distance finders" should be allowed in competition (as strokesavers and advice from caddies are allowed)?

— *Gordon, Cumbernauld*

Where the hell is Cumbernauld? I think I may have exposed myself there once after a tournament.

I think absolutely *anything* that helps a person score better should be allowed. You should be able to fire flaming arrows into the back of your opponent, use a dwarf as a sand wedge, check with the blimpcam to ascertain where your errant shot may have gone, have séances in the locker room, and use naked exotic dancers as caddies. It's all about ratings for me now.

A Load of C. R. (A. A.) A. P.

M y Dearest Garfield:

As you know, I have long dreamed of owning a TV station and starting my own religion, but it has occurred to me recently that the fulfillment of my yearning may have, for all these years, been sitting right under my very own nose. Of course, given the size and volume of the appendage in question, I feel somewhat justified in cutting myself a little slack for not having noticed it, but no matter. Let us move on to the matter at hand.

At the time of this writing, you are the only living soul who has any knowledge whatsoever of my grand plan, and, of course (unless you have already read the end of this letter), even you are clueless, which is precisely why I have chosen you to be my best friend and brain caddie.

What I'm talking about here is the formation of "Comrades for the Removal (and Also) Abolition of Par," or C.R. (A.A.) A.P., to you and me. (Though I think it might be best to leave out the two A's in the middle; I mean, the last thing we need to do is attract people who don't drink.)

Let's face it, these days the whole concept of par is about as useful as an ashtray on a motorcycle, and it has clearly become irrelevant to all except those who feel miffed by the continuing improvement of equipment, which allows top players everywhere to look even more windswept and dashing, as they reach par fives with swashbuckling abandon.

I would go it alone, but this is for the benefit of the ordinary man in the fairway, and as you know I'm not nearly ordinary enough. Come to think of it, you're seldom in the fairway either, but on behalf of every golfer, Tour pro, or hacker—man, woman, or child—I am saying that enough is enough, and for that matter, it's quite sufficient, too. No longer will we be brutalized into calling a 500-yard hole a "par four" simply because some chinless, absurdly rich, Ivy-League half-wit in paisley underpants, sock-garters, and a trilby wants to make par "relevant."

Now, I don't need to tell a former male flight attendant and accomplished gopher-angler such as yourself that throughout the course of history, mankind has suffered much at the hands of man-unkind, but as you know, occasionally there has been a time when the vile suppression of the proletariat exploded into an uncontrollable backlash. It only takes one man to change the course of history, but that man must be able to capture the hearts and minds of the ordinary person, and today, my friend, that man is you. This is our chance to take control of the game, and the way to go about it is through the mind-control device already in place, known as The Golf Channel.

Uh-huh, you read me right, I said, The Golf Channel. First, we hypnotize Peter Kessler, then we break onto the set of "Golf Talk Live," and get him to take over. I have several phone drones in place to feed him the new Rules info, and with his mesmerizing voice, it should be only a matter of time before we have the switchboard lighting up like the crowd at a Grateful Dead concert.

We tell them it's time to level the playing field and give everyone on every golf course the same card on the first tee. It should have the number 100 printed in the center, with room for three underlined digits below. This would be the total amount of shots hit by the competitor, which would be subtracted from 100 at the completion of play, leaving a gross score, to which a handicap could be added. The higher the number, the better the score. Bob's your uncle, Fanny's your Aunt, it's as simple as that.

I can see us standing on the tapestry-draped balcony right now, you and me, bathing in the adoration with our hands outstretched over the seething masses. I can hear your oratory now.

"Come to us, all of you, and bring us your sick (the sicker the better), your wounded (we have a deal with E-Z-Go), your dispirited (the bar is open), and more importantly, your cash, credit cards, and checkbooks. Yes, make no mistake; we need money to do this. Like Bono, the God we believe in isn't short of cash, but unlike that singing, self-righteous, whining, hypocritical blowhole, we haven't got a flattened nickel to scratch our small dog's backside with, and we're going to need some serious moolah to get this movement up and running. So cough it up, you bastards, and before you know it, a six may be an eagle depending on where you live."

(I know that makes no sense, but if you hold a clipboard and say it loud enough with a pencil behind your ear, trust me, it won't matter.)

Where was I? Oh, yes, I was going to mention why it will work. For centuries, the ordinary golfer has been spectacularly underrepresented when it comes to making the Rules for the game. All we have to do is dangle out an oversize carrot with a spring onion-like effect like this and they'll chase us all the way to the bank.

Gazza, hang on to your handlebars and listen to me. If we get enough live bodies in this first draft, we may never need to worry about numbers again (and I mean off the golf course, too), but you must promise me you won't go designing your own uniform or anything.

Please, I know how you love to do it, but it's the first sign of madness in a leader, and for the love of Tiger Woods on a scooter, it's not like you need to advertise at the best of times. I'm sorry, but if we're going to abolish par, we have to be taken seriously. No jodhpurs, no riding crop, definitely nothing in spandex, and since Noriega, the Tommy Bahama look is a no-no, too. I don't care how much they pay you, we don't need you looking like some 15-handicap Guatemalan banana magnate.

No, take my word for it, and think about Idi Amin, Saddam Hussein, or maybe Mohammar Qaddafi. If the feathers on that desert dingbat's epaulettes were standard issue, the rest of the Libyan armed forces would be working in Vegas as showgirls. Our George the Second's driveway may not go all the way to his garage, but I'll bet his suits are Brooks Brothers. Bless his cotton socks from Target, this is the greatest country in the world, and this is going to work! I can feel it in your water. I'm thinking we need simple shirts for this, maybe in UPS brown, although in the back of my mind I have the feeling it's been done before.

The next thing we need to do is kidnap George Peper, the evil commander-in-chief of the very publication I am using as a facade for the entire operation. He's an agreeable sort and fairly tight with the Wizard of Far Hills, Short Hills, Poppy Hills, or wherever, so he's familiar with the layout of the "Big Bunker." He's just had both wheels retreaded, so it shouldn't be a big job getting the daft old gimp on a gurney. We'll put on a couple of surgeon's masks and you can tell him one of those "oscopy" stories of yours that frighten even me. That ought to do it. If we keep enough Scotch in him, it'll be a dawdle to get a few of my vitriolic magazine pieces attributed to him and start an internal row in the Bunker.

Over at St. Andy's, the Royal & Ancients already have their niblicks in a knot over this restitutionalized coefficient debacle with the boys in the Bunker, so all we have to do is slip one daft idea into their heads and I guarantee you at least a thousand of them will come out. Natural allies, my arse. At the height of the bickering, we suddenly appear with our one-page rulebook and a column of Bethpage lunatics behind us. All we have to do is promise them a game at Pine Valley and bingo! The game is ours.

Keep it under your helmet old boy, there's more where this came from.

Nudge, nudge, wink, wink.

First of all, I would like to say thank you for the countless laughs. I recently read your book *Somewhere in Ireland, a Village Is Missing an Idiot*, and I have to say that although many may disregard your insight for the game, I think you are a well-spoken man with great opinions. What is it like to be able to see all of the greatest courses, and can you recommend any courses to absolutely avoid?

— *Cody Powers, Gallatin, Tennessee*

Anyone who questions my insight into the game is someone to be avoided at all costs. It is obvious to even the most casual observer that my studied, well-formulated, and keenly presented opinions are irrefutable and carry the weight of a Papal Bull, which, as we all know, cannot be questioned by secular authority, including Tim Finchem, David Fay, or Dick Cheney.

My list of courses to avoid:

1. Any course in North America that names its holes. (And don't worry about Augusta, you ain't playing there anyway.)

2. Courses anywhere that contain any reference to devil worship in their name, e.g., Devil's Ridge, Beelzebub's Butt, Mephastrophie's Meadows, etc.

3. Anything designed by Arthur Hills. Eva and Adolf would have committed suicide three months earlier had they been in one of his bunkers.

We're Not Worthy

I was down in the Cayman Islands last week with my wife and baby daughter, both of whom must be obeyed at all times, enjoying a little R&R on the beach. I am not a pretty sight in a swimsuit, I can tell you, although you will be glad to know I opted for a voluminous pair of baggies, rather than the old banana hammock, marble bag, grape smuggler, or whatever you want to call those despicable spandex loincloths which are so popular with the big-willied continental types that we all love to laugh at and secretly despise.

Good Lord, that was a little more than I had intended to share with you, but let's press on regardless, shall we? So anyway, I'm lying there like some albino manatee with a tanned face and flippers, hoping to avoid the ocean altogether for fear of being harpooned by a passing Japanese trawler, when I am—horror of horrors—recognized by a tanned and buff stranger in, wouldn't you know it, a snakeskin posing pouch. Before this man opens his mouth, I hate him, his ancestors, and any offspring he might have. I have issues here, okay?

"I thought you'd be at St. Andrews," says Mr. Look-at-my-sausage.

"No, that's a Disney telecast," I said dryly, looking at his sausage.

"Oh yeah, Johnny Miller and Gary McCord...those guys, huh?"

"Yeah, those guys, and John Madden."

"Whoa, no kiddin', he's doin' golf now?"

So I look at him over my sunglasses, and he figures it out. He knows that I know that he only stopped here to look at my wife, who is the most beautiful woman on the beach, and is wearing even less spandex than him. The fact that he recognized me seemed at the time to be an excuse to loiter, but not anymore. Like most iron pumpers, he is 5-foot-4 on a thick rug, and I know I can barge him into the tide and drown him in cellulite.

"Hey, enjoy the rest of your holiday," he says, and minces off. Satisfied that I am still the dominant male, I go back to being only mildly pissed off.

I guess it's due to the fact that I've spent most of my life squinting into the sun, but I have a really low threshold for sunbathing. I get antsy really quickly. So during the course of the vacation, I found myself making frequent visits to the old gogglebox and listening to the dulcet tones of Strange and Alliss and company, whom I thought did a great job.

What a rare treat it was to see the Old Course play as it did. Bump and run, dunch and trundle, hop, skip, and jump. Players reading the fairways 50 yards short of the greens. Bunkers with gravitational pull, and the extraordinary beauty of the links at dusk, when the swales and hollows are cloaked in shadow, and mineshaft darkness fills the sandy craters. I adore St. Andrews. There are more spectacular courses in golf, but none has the enigmatic mystery, the sensual lure, or the hallowed graveyard aura of the first, and the greatest of them all. I remember every shot I ever hit there, and I hit quite a few.

Some will say that the scoring was too low, the course too easy for the modern game. But the truth is, Tiger didn't win by playing the modern game; he played the ancient game, along the ground, magically transforming himself into half man, half sheep, all brilliance. A great golf course is a canvas upon which the great player can display his artistry, and we are lucky enough to be witnessing a renaissance in our sport. If the golfing gods exist, surely the golf equivalent of the ceiling of the Sistine Chapel will never be altered. Fortunately, the R&A seem to be of the same opinion.

I laughed out loud reading about the gut-wrenching, butt-cheek-clenching fear that, even for a professional athlete, can be fostered by the belief that somehow "I don't belong here" or "I'm not good enough to be the Open champion." Do you think that things might have been different for you had you worked with a sports psychologist who could have helped you with the tornado watches issued on Sundays for the areas including the western region of your mental health and the northern portion of your ability to deal rationally with your disconcerted precarious emotional situation? What's your opinion of tour players using shrinks?

—— *David, Richmond, Virginia*

I have no problem with those guys using shrinks. There are some seriously deranged people out there, and a lot of them need those mental colonoscopies. Mac O'Grady was on the cutting edge of "The Twilight Zone" for a number of years. Remember what he said, and I'm paraphrasing here, "Wish I was a Kellogg's corn flake, floatin' in my bowl takin' movies. Relaxin' awhile, living in style, talking to a raisin who occasionally plays L.A. Casually glancin' at his toupee. Wish I was an English muffin, 'bout to make the most out of a toaster. I'd ease myself down, coming up brown. I prefer boysenberry more than any ordinary jam." (Apologies to Paul Simon.)

If I had worked with a sports psychologist the poor devil would be making wallets in Switzerland right now.

I'm Marrying Tiger

She-Who-Must-Be-Obeyed doesn't normally allow me to address the subject of marriage in this column (or anywhere else, for that matter). But given these extraordinary times, I have been granted 750 words. In my capacity as a newly ordained minister, I have been asked to perform the sacred rites of marriage between Tiger Woods and the unbearably lovely Elin Nordegren. Yes, my tiny flock, I am now Rear Cardinal of the brand-spanking-new Hasidic Presbycatholic Church of St. Arnold-on-the-Green (none of the fun, all of the guilt, but half the price). I ordained myself online last Thursday, my kit arrived today and I am *sooo* excited. I've got a two-foot-tall red conehead cap; an infallibility headcover for my oversized Cobra crosier; a skin-tight sans-a-belt cassock with matching V-neck intarsia surplice; and a righteous indignation that would make Jimmy Swaggart stop crying and drop the collection plate.

Why have I been chosen? Privacy, of course. You could have gagged me with a hamster when that rotten gnu-herder at his tawdry little zoo in South Africa dropped a dime on T and E (Who-Must-Soon-Be-Obeyed). If I weren't a man of the cloth, I'd wish a pox on the dirty bastard. Over the past few years, I have always done my utmost to protect the privacy of the world's greatest golfer, deliberately tripping Golf Channel cameramen, keeping my interview questions short and pointless. I've even avoided eye contact for fear of learning something about Tiger that might later be tortured out of me. Hell, I once kissed Roger Maltbie on the lips and held him firmly by his microphone to keep him away from Tiger. Greater love hath no announcer than he who tastes secondhand Marlboros and Michelob Ultra for his friend. Mine is a noble cause, and watching Tiger play has been, until now, my only reward. Due totally to the fact that I know absolutely nothing about him, I now regard myself as his closest friend in the media. Deep joy!

Naturally, every horrible hack has an opinion on how the ball and chain will affect Tiger's career, but I am not going to speculate. I'm not the average sports journalist, who thinks people might actually give a rat's ass what he writes. I know better than that. I prefer to use my tried and trusted system: Wait and see what happens, then claim I predicted it. In fact, I forecasted Tiger's wedding in these pages three months ago, in my Fearless '04Cast. Okay, so I said he'd marry Barbara Nicklaus—I was close.

Elin's appearance on the scene was a challenge to my relationship with Tiger, but again I took the high road and chose not to be there. There was far too much risk that Elin might fall for me instead (she's only human), and as She-Who-Must points out (she's writing this bit) I already signed a scorecard on this one, don't want to die, etc. Fortunately, in order to maintain the special relationship between Tiger and me, I've gone out of my way not to meet his new bride.

Now, I can imagine the furor this news will cause among the scumbag paparazzi, but I can state quite categorically that they can all go photo themselves. The date of these historic nuptials—unspecified by Tiger and Elin—has been left up to me, and I would never tell. I've already forgotten. However, I can let the location slip. Try getting your horrible little helicopters to hover over a diving bell 300 feet below the surface somewhere in the South Pacific, media vermin! And don't think you'll catch sight of the Very Rev. Rear Cardinal, either. Respecting the privacy of his friends as always, he won't be there. The Church of St. Arnold-on-the-Green is a low-maintenance outfit, so I'll just leave the happy couple a note in Latin:

For Tiger and Elin, on their wedding day—

Icto alterno semper lude et nil desperandum (Always play alternate shot and don't let the bastards get you down).

Love,

Cardinal Dave

All I hear about Tiger is that his swing change is almost there. My question is, why change when you were the best in the world by no slim margin?

— James

Because golf is a never-ending journey, not a destination. My God, I'm deep today!

In your opinion, what weaknesses do you see in Tiger's game? I cannot find any—wondering what your thoughts are?

— Kevin, Chicago, Illinois

Are you kidding me? The Tigers lost 119 games last season, Kevin. Christ, one more and they would have set a record for the most losses in a single season. They have no pitching, they can't hit... no weaknesses???

Huh? Oh... sorry, you mean Tiger Woods. You're right, he's pretty buttoned-up, golf-wise, I mean. He'll be fine as long as he maintains his self-discipline and doesn't "Kobe" up or get a gigantic tattoo on his face or something. I would advise him not to make too many more commercials with Charles Barkley, though, it might start rubbing off.

The Thin Men

I s it my imagination, or is golf being taken over by the anorexic? Of the entire field at the Mercedes, only Hal Sutton could be described as "not thin," and even he isn't close to fat. Why, even Mark Calcavecchia has gotten thin, the scoundrel. Davis Love has a little bit of a Nelly Kelly going on there, but he's still tall enough to look like a one-iron that swallowed a golf ball.

Where have all the fat guys gone? People like Tim Herron and Big John Daly are becoming an endangered species out there—so much so, that I think we may eventually have to have them darted, crated up, and sent somewhere to see if we can breed them in captivity.

But really, Jack used to be tubby; Casper and Ed "Porky" Oliver were positively spherical; and Julius Boros and Lionel Hebert both loved their grub. There are five corpulent competitors off the top of my head. We had exactly none in the field last week. Maybe we should give everybody a cart.

Off and running would be a fair description of Sergio Garcia, I suppose, after his victory in the season opener. Running, jumping, skipping, gripping, gripping, gripping stuff. I'm led to believe the little ratbag may be scribbling in the mag too, along with that other sniper's nightmare, Charles Howell the third of my weight.

Just when they thought they were done with homework. We'll see how they'll shape up now that they're journalists. It's the first step on the slippery downward staircase toward stretch marks and mediastinal shift, let's hope.

Tiger's not exactly obese, but he's looking positively tubby by comparison to the new wave, most of whom would fall into their boxers if they lifted their arms up. Something needs to be done before a caddie accidentally puts a headcover on his player, and sticks him in the bag beside the 3-wood. I'd write to the commissioner about it, if he didn't weigh 140 pounds with his glasses on. I think he's in on the conspiracy.

There is some kind of liposuction going on in the fitness trailer or something, which might be why they don't allow the media in there. (Of course, most of the media wouldn't fit in there.)

Thank God for announcers like Roger Maltbie, Peter Alliss, and me. Real men with breasts who have the decency to feel rotten most mornings, who always wear a shirt, and never, ever sunbathe. Just yesterday I took the skin off the roof of my mouth with a corn chip smothered with molten cheese. When was the last time David Duval did that? (Actually, one of the really annoying things about David is that he eats like a seagull, so he's probably not a great example, but no matter. I'm trying to piss off skinny people here.)

One of the great things about the game of golf, which sets it apart from other professional sports, is that the people who love to watch the game are still actually involved in playing it, so they can identify with the players. It used to be that in the galleries at PGA Tour events, the big guys wearing the chilidogs had someone to point at, and felt an affinity.

These days, they have to watch an LPGA event to get the same warm feeling, and I don't know what it is, but there's something not right about that. (Not that it makes them bad people, mind you.)

Since the Masters ended, I've been constantly searching for news on the Sergio Garcia "attitude" toward interviewers. I haven't found a single comment. I don't know if it's a matter of no one in the media wanting to explore it or what. What are your views regarding what's going on with Sergio's attitude? He seemed to indicate it's a "Tiger gets all the press" thing, but I can't imagine it's that simple.

— *Ric Holland, Loganville, Georgia*

You don't own that tunnel in New York, do you? Man, that's got to be a moneymaker for you.

Isn't it funny how when players puke in their shoes and play like ten handicappers, they don't want to talk to anybody? Then when things turn around and they shoot lights out, "the press guys are a bunch of derelicts who only want to cover the leaders and no one cared when I was shooting 11 over and to hell with you bastards and I don't have to talk to you 'cause you're not the boss of me and anyway, I don't like you and I'm going to my room now and never, ever like have to talk to you like EVER again and I'm gonna hold my breath till I burst. That'll teach you, you geeks! I HATE TIGER! I HATE HIM, I HATE HIM!"

Other than that, I think Sergio behaved in a very mature manner.

The Life and Crimes of Heavy D

This was a tough one to write. I was with John Daly for the last two rounds and the playoff hole at the Buick Invitational, and it was all I could do not to root for him on the air. Lucky my mike was closed when he hit that tournament-winning sand shot in the playoff—I was screaming, "GO ON, FAT BOY, GO ON!" I just love the guy, and if his galleries are anything to go by, I'm not alone. I suppose I could do the right thing and attempt some semblance of objectivity, but at the end of the day I'm a golf fan, and there aren't many of those who are unhappy to see the return of John Daly.

Golf has had a few greats, some of whom have been a little reality challenged or even totally f---ed up, but compared with John Belushi—sorry, John *Daly* (Freudian slip) —they all look like choirboys. (With the possible exception of Tom Weisk--f.) But this is a love story, not a fearless expose. That's right, JD's life is a soap opera, minus the bad plot, crap acting, great makeup and, of course, the suave, handsome, sophisticated hero.

The bottom line is that we *luuuve* this big boy like one of our own because that's what he is. You see, I believe every honest soul among us has a little Johnny inside, some nasty little character parasite that we struggle to suppress but that aches to take us over and expose us. Mine is an addiction to Bushmills, coupled with a pathological fear of Bill Murray. Heaven forbid anyone should discover our dark little weaknesses or hear our inner squeals for help. Johnny's flaw isn't so little though, and not very well hidden. No, we're talking about a guy with a crack the size of the Grand Canyon. (Plus a smaller one that pops out every now and then as he bends to pick the ball out of the hole.) That big ol' crevice in JD's disordered personality is held together with gaffer's tape, chewing gum, quiet desperation, Diet Coke, and nicotine, and it looks like it could burst at any time, exposing the hairy, scary black hole of the big lad's innermost nowhere. Sports fans are a little evil, you know—we watch because we want to see a crash, and we don't mind serious injury as long as there's a survivor to ogle afterward.

Call him what you will, but Johnny's one hell of a survivor.

I knew him when he weighed 160 pounds and his mullet was just a guppy. I was leading an event in Africa by a shot after three rounds and was introduced to him on the first tee. He hit it so far past me that day, he had to wave me up several times, and he wound up beating me by one stroke. Who knew this lunatic would win the PGA and the Open Championship? He has married himself out of a couple of fortunes, almost died of his enthusiasms, and made an album for Wal-Mart. And the only reason he's never tossed himself off a tall building is that, with his record on personal decisions, he'd probably land on someone he loved.

Johnny hasn't won more because he has always had a habit of letting the crowd choose the club for him. And that would be the driver—people don't come to see Long John lay up, and he's never disappointed them. Whether he crashes in flames or lands perfectly, he's always giving value.

We're talking about a guy who won the Open Championship at *St. Andrews*, man! Same place our favorite big, fat sinner was seen at the 1993 Dunhill Cup, sitting on the steps of the Royal & Ancient clubhouse with tattered jeans hanging out of battered rain pants, chewing a burger right out of a McDonald's wrapper. The Claret Jug he won there in 95 has often been filled with beer, champagne, and occasionally even claret, but I guarantee you only Daly would get ketchup on it.

And don't think John is just a champion for the common man. His win this year at Torrey Pines made him a hero and a symbol of hope for the millions of Americans who are held hostage by addiction or united by that lowest of common denominators: the horrifying disease of depression. Whether you live in a refrigerator carton under the interstate or you're the chairman of the greens committee, John Daly is an inspiration to you or someone close to you. He is to me. So let's bless his giant liver, his even bigger heart, and his huge, fat ass while we're at it, for John Daly is a good man, a kind man, and a brave man, and we are lucky to be seeing him do more than just survive on the PGA Tour.

Hi D: What's with the fancy goatee? Your shaver break? Why don't you play anymore? I seem to remember you challenging back in the day. Didn't you even win one? It'd be great to see you and McCord coming down the 18th tied for the U.S. Senior Open. Oops, are you even 50? Last question. Why doesn't the PGA allow a more relaxed dress code? You know how gross it is to watch guys sweating like Shaq walk around my television screen? Yettch! How about nice dress shorts like the ladies wear? I bet the scores would even go lower with more comfortable attire. Take it easy. Love your ironic insight.

— *Fred Rogger, British Columbia, Canada*

Have you considered decaf? And don't address me as "D." Where do you live, in the bar scene from "Star Wars"? To answer your questions in order, the goatee hides one of my chins, I hate golf, I won ten, and the reason no one takes the U.S. Amateur seriously is because they're allowed to wear shorts. It looks like a high school event. Go get a bunch of paper towels and then imagine John Daly in a nice pair of dress shorts like the ladies wear. Yettch!

Aliens

As I write, I'm speeding toward Atlanta at 29,000 feet in a big Fokker, and right now I know more about the Atlanta Athletic Club than Tiger Woods, because I've been there once before, to shoot a feature about Jerry Pate. Okay, so I only saw the last hole, and all I did was simulate peeing on the plaque, which commemorates his great second shot in the '75 U.S. Open. I'll give you that, but still, it gives me a little more local knowledge than the favorite this week.

I interviewed Tiger last Friday in Orlando, for our PGA preview show, which aired before the third round of the Buick in Flint. I like Flint, because it reminds me of my native Belfast in that you can drift off to sleep at night, lulled by the gentle sound of automatic gunfire in the distance. Ah, the memories.

The thing is, though, I wasn't meant to be in Orlando last Friday, at least not until Tiger withdrew from the Buick and decided to bunk up at home instead. The next thing you know, the golf world is turned upside down.

I was supposed to interview the lad on Wednesday, and work the cable shows on Thursday and Friday, which worked perfectly, as I had to do a charity day on Tuesday in Sarnia, Canada, just over the border from Detroit. I was working in a decidedly logical and linear fashion, so I should have known something was about to wad up my shorts.

Tiger withdraws, and the next thing I know I'm on another miserable Fokker to Orlando. McCord, who had planned to spend a couple of days wearing tight leather shorts and yodeling magnificently outside his mobile home in Vail, is buried for two bonus days under the lip of the ashtray in his nonsmoking room at the lovely Holiday Inn Flint.

It's the chaos theory at work. A butterfly flaps its wings in the equatorial jungle of Zaire, an elderly lady breaks wind in Scunthorpe, England, and a small boy in Floydata, Texas, runs out of puff in the middle of a trombone solo. It's all connected, trust me.

Anyway, that's my side of this sordid little tale, but here's a day in the life of the defending champion. Last Friday, he started his day with a bowl of Fruit & Fiber, and a short drive in a Porsche 911 Turbo, from his house to the clubhouse at Isleworth.

Third gear was flirted with only briefly, and he was alone, so no underwear was personalized. There, he met with an overweight, hungover, and extremely flatulent announcer who asked him a dozen questions, all of which he answered correctly.

In the adjoining room, there were a number of people who spent a not inconsiderable time setting up three large tables with a vast quantity of high-quality photos of Woods and enough flags to identify every asteroid in our galaxy as a colony of planet Major.

After I got done with him, he signed two thousand items with a pen that filmed his actual hand, in the process of writing his actual signature. Then he hit balls for the rest of the day and went home in the aforementioned four-wheeled mode of vehicular transport. I don't know what he did when he got there, because we're not that close, but I will tell you this: whatever it was, I guarantee it wasn't human.

He's an alien, I'm telling you. I know you've heard me say it before, but if he's human, then where is the equivalent female? Ha! Got you all there.

I'm starting to worry a little about David Duval, too. When he broke out of the crowd at the British Open and took off those reentry shields, or whatever they are, he looked like that blind guy in Star Trek—you know, the one that wears the air filter on his head.

Don't say you weren't warned. It's all part of an elaborate plan to take over the planet, and if I didn't know any better, I'd say McCord might be involved, too. Watch closely, it could be the start of something big.

I've been following golf coverage for a couple of years now and I really like what you do on the CBS team. You and McCord are the best ever, man!!! Here's my question: Who are you a bigger fan of, Tiger or Phil?

— *Sergio Montiel, New York, NY*

I can't decide whether I prefer Tiger or Phil, or for that matter Ernie. I like 'em all for different reasons. Tiger's got intensity, drive, intelligence, and extremely rare focusing power. Phil's personable, self-effacing, possesses uncanny skill with a wedge, likes to gamble, and will stand there for two hours and sign autographs until the very last kid leaves. Ernie is a big friendly giant, and if he ever gave a rat's ass he could probably beat the other two's best ball. Maybe we could combine them and call it Tigernie MickELSon. Those three would be a fine pair, if ever I saw one.

Phil!

I don't want to come off as a genius here, but I did predict this one. In a CBS promo shot way before the Masters (you've seen it by now), I prayed for Phil Mickelson to win a major. At the end you saw that my jammies and sheets were festooned with Phil faces. Ha ha, that's a wrap, end of script. But I didn't like it.

"Ye faithless Philistines," said I. "Phil will win!" Now, others may tell you I actually said, "might maybe just possibly" instead of "will." The point is, I made them shoot an alternate ending, thanking the golf gods for a Mickelson victory.

I almost lost faith on Sunday. It looked like the usual Sunday afternoon at the Masters: The leaders went out, and Phil started knocking nails into his own coffin with a big left-handed hammer. He wasn't the only one on the funeral march, either. Until Ernie Els's eagle on 8, the whole show was looking like a train wreck. And who should emerge but Mr. 0-for-46-in-the-Majors?

I can't remember a major in which a leader faltered so badly, then regained his momentum. That takes some serious subcutaneous heart, but Phil's demeanor was positively beatific all day. Even when he flubbed his second bunker shot of the day, at the 5th, there was no dismay. Rather, there was a centered, almost blissed-out look about the big man, and finally, when Chris DiMarco's bunker shot trickled over his marker and came to rest about an inch behind it on the 18th green, giving

Mickelson a perfect read, you just felt it was Phil's day.

The atmosphere over the last few holes was crackling like the top of the mast above Frankenstein's lab. Phil didn't blink, not even when he stared at the scoreboard after Ernie's eagle at 13. There was a roar, then a number changed on a scoreboard, and then another roar. Again and again it happened. After Phil went through the 15th hole, I stayed in my tower there, riveted to the monitor. Fans all over the golf course were gathering beneath camera towers, waiting for news, wanting the roars and cheers they were hearing translated into whos and hows. Our cameramen turned their cameras around so the fans below could watch the action on tiny 6-by-4-inch black-and-white viewfinders. Augusta National had never seen anything like it. Martha Burk could have run naked down Washington Road and people would have paid her even less attention than they did last year. This was about Phil.

It was Guinness-ad brilliant, that's how good it was. In the week of Arnold Palmer's 50th and last Masters, it was exit one people's champion and enter the next, landing flat on his big, awkward feet on the greatest stage in golf. Phil doesn't hitch his pants as much as Arnie did, but his connection with fans is the same. His win was one of the biggest sports moments of the new century, maybe the biggest, and it laid to rest the notion that golf can't generate a buzz without Tiger Woods. If Tiger is the new Jack Nicklaus, Phil's the modern Arnie.

I always figured he was going to win a major no matter what. As well as he played in them three straight thirds at Augusta at the very least someone was bound to brain-fart the lead away and he'd be there to catch it. But nobody fainted and handed him this one. When it mattered most, Phil beat Els, a great front-runner at the peak of his game, and he did it with his head and his heart. His win was golf's best clutch performance since Bobby Jones won the 1930 U.S. Amateur at Merion to complete the Grand Slam. Sure, there was Nicklaus at Augusta in '86, but Jack wasn't the "Best Player Never to Have Won a Major."

It's fitting that Arnold's last major was Phil's first win. They both play the way most people would like to, with bollocks-to-it-I'm-only-here-once abandon. This time it was all swash and no buckle for Phil. With King Kong finally off his back, he might really go deep now. Hogan was 34 when he won his first major, and he went on to win eight more. Phil turns 34 on June 16th. If he wins a slew of majors, there'll be roars of joy all over the place.

Fans may look at Tiger with awe, but they look at Phil with love. Because it's just golf after all, and the truth of it is we all believe we can pull off that crazy shot or stare down the winning putt and knock it in. Like Phil Mickelson, we might fall short 46 times in a row, but we only need to get it right once to prove that sometimes, just when we need it most, the golf gods hear our prayers.

David, my friends and I were discussing Phil Mickelson's Masters win and have reached a disagreement we were hoping you could settle. Just prior to Phil's winning putt, DiMarco had to putt along the same line as Phil. When DiMarco putted his ball, Phil quickly ran behind DiMarco to watch how his putt reacted. Though legal, I found the action very unprofessional and ungentleman-like and never have witnessed this action prior to this (not even playing with hackers on the weekend). My friends disagree and state, "Anything to win." What do you think?

— *Robert Genetelli, Wantage, New Jersey*

Come on now Bobby, how many guys called you "Genetalia," in high school?

Well, let's think about this… I'm the best player never to win a major… all I have to do is make this putt… the damn Masters, for God's sake… finally, a MAJOR… after all this time… Mr. Palmer's last Masters… everybody's pulling for me… should I look at this putt to see what it does??? Noooooo, that would be rude. People will think me impolite, for God's sake! What would Emily Post say? The boys at La Jolla Country Club will be appalled. OR… I could lose this thing. Yeah, I'm checking it out!

Phil's actions were not only legal, they were as professional as it gets.

Smoke 'Em If You've Got 'Em

I have long been convinced that you can tell a player's personality by the way he swings a golf club. A case in point is Fred Couples, whose swing is easygoing, comfortable, and even downright lovable at times. Then there's John Daly, whose swing is immensely enjoyable to watch, but there is way too much of it. Nick Price is classic type A—quick, powerful, and to the point—and Colin Montgomerie swings very carefully, with a strangely irritating follow-through. Craig Stadler's swing says, "This is me, and up yours if you don't like it."

A week or so ago, I was on my way back from Greensboro, when everyone was startled by a sudden loud rasping noise from inside the plane. I was sitting with Stadler at the time, so naturally I thought nothing of it. But then it happened a couple more times, and the flight attendant walked down the aisle with his head cocked to one side, as if he were listening for a squirrel in one of the air conditioners. This, in my experience, when combined with a few loud whining noises and a couple of violent bumps, has seldom been a good sign, but workaholic that I am, I decided to keep a close eye on the action, so that should we survive, I could report back to my readers. So with that in mind, I settled in to observe Craig's behavior during the crisis, as we bumped, rasped, and whined toward doom, or DFW Airport.

True to form, he looked at me as if he had just lipped out from three feet. "This is pretty typical," he said. "I suppose we're all going to die now. That'd be about right."

"My God," I thought. "I'm in a metal tube, 35,000 feet above the ground, sitting next to Eeyore!"

It was in that moment, though, that I knew everything would be all right, because no matter what happens to Eeyore, no matter how bad, he always comes out of it okay. As for my own part in this near tragedy, I felt more like Rabbit. "Just my luck," I thought. "I'm going to be in a plane wreck, and I'm sitting next to Stadler, right after he loses 50 pounds. Six months ago, he might have been some use as an airbag."

Hey, Eeyore might have lost the playoff on Sunday in Houston, but that's okay, everybody loves Eeyore.

Fall

The Unholy One

Sadly, Ben Hogan and I have but one thing in common: We share a birthday on August 13. Ben is dearly departed and I am unfortunately turning 40, which is convincing me that my ambition of becoming Hogan is drawing ever nearer to reality.

Thanks to these pages, the southward migration of my gray hair is now well known and, dear reader, I must report that other things are deteriorating, as well. As I write, a dripping tap in the bathroom is causing an uncontrollable urge. The good news is that the repeated trips down the hall during the night are serving as my only decent exercise these days.

The cause was a minor swelling in the old wedding tackle, in a place that doesn't normally swell. That sent me off to the doc faster than a Nick Price backswing, but thankfully the diagnosis was a case of inappropriate underwear combined with a 36-hole walk. (Thanks to medical science, I now realize I am infinitely better off with tennis elbow than golf ball.)

In a word, I have become increasingly aware of my own mortality and am trying to justify my existence on the planet, which is most unlike me.

But I appear to be in the minority, especially among some

of the tournament winners in professional golf. I am hearing in more and more of players' acceptance speeches that they could not have prevailed without divine intervention.

So, I figure, as one who was always more inclined to credit myself with my successes and blame the Almighty for any failures, that it is my bound duty as a course reporter to investigate further.

I am, of course, aware of the sensitive nature of this subject. Many of you will dismiss me as a blasphemous scoundrel, with no notion of matters of the soul.

You might be right, although I have experience to show otherwise. You might call me a lapsed Episcobuddatheist, but please take into account that I grew up in Northern Ireland where an idiot who doesn't even go to church is liable to shoot you because he thinks his religion is better than yours. People have forgotten the message and worship the creed.

It seems to me that wherever in the world you find unrest, someone's religion or philosophy is behind it. There is no more dangerous person in the world than one who thinks only he can be right.

Of course, I could be wrong.

The way I look at it, golf is like a decent religion. They are both based on honesty, love, tolerance, and respect—for one's self and others. The only major difference is, in golf no groveling is involved. (With one exception, of course—when the ball teeters on the edge of the hole, groveling to the Almighty is compulsory.)

You can, if you want to stretch a bit, draw parallels between a church and a golf course, in that the Lord's name is invoked frequently in both areas, albeit for entirely opposite reasons.

Which is why I am all in favor of every man of the cloth taking up his clubs and walking with us in the name of golf. (Smite the ball with thy rod or thy staff, verily I say unto thee.) They would all soon learn, with the greatest of reverence, that this is a holy game played by mortal men, which, at times, would make a bishop punch the nearest nun.

The finest example of this truth was shown to me by, of all people, a Catholic priest.

Father Francis Hogue was a sweet-natured man who embodied everything good and kind about his profession. He was a parish priest who had time for everyone, just so long as they didn't mind meeting him down at the bookie's or in the bar at the golf club.

I once asked him how he reconciled his drinking and gambling with the pastoral aspect of his life. "Davey, my boy," he answered, "it's never a sin, just as long as you don't enjoy it!" Needless to say, I loved him from that moment on.

He had a darker side, though, which only manifested itself between the first tee and the 18th green. He normally shot between 110 and 130, but on one glorious Monday morning he hit a hot streak that was reminiscent of the scene with the bishop in *Caddyshack*.

Luigi Esdale, the club's assistant pro, and I were along as witnesses and as the day unfolded, it looked as if he might break 90. But over the last few holes, he choked majestically, becoming angrier and angrier until he reached the last green with a 20-footer for a 98.

His first putt was a sniveling yip that finished some five feet short. Stonefaced, he set up over the next one and as the tension mounted, I noticed that his jugular vein had become knotted and ropelike.

After what seemed like an eternity, he made an epileptic spasm with the putter and the ball wobbled to the edge of the hole, where it teetered insolently. He threw his hands in the air, his fingers slashing and clawing at the clouds as he dropped to his knees, turning his now purple face heavenward.

He drew a giant breath and, like a werewolf, howled at the top of his voice, "Jesus, Mary, and Joseph!!!!!" A few seconds passed and Luigi and I looked at each other, slack-jawed and silent, as Father Hogue turned his murderous gaze to the ball and then back upward.

Once again he filled his lungs and screamed, "And, the wee donkey, too!!!!!" Afterward he buried his face in his hands.

The ball crept agonizingly forward, then lurched into the hole. The sound of it rattling into the cup snapped Father Frank out of his funk and he knelt bolt upright, staring at the hole in disbelief.

I have never seen a man's expression change from thunderous purple anger to chalk-faced guilt so fast in all my life. He had waited more than 10 seconds before the ball fell in, but call us old-fashioned, Luigi and I didn't call a penalty on him and the good father had his 99.

The more astute of you may have determined by now that I am not exactly what you would call a devout anything. I do, however, have the greatest respect for anyone who can find peace of mind in the religion or philosophy of his choosing while still retaining the ability to tolerate and even embrace others who choose to be different.

I know I have plenty of things to be thankful for, not the least of which is the gift of my own personal guardian angel—my wife, Anita. She is a devout church member, so I go with her. Frankly, if she is going to insist on surrounding herself with sinners, I'd at least like to be the one standing next to her.

Just the other day, we went to hear the archbishop of Canterbury (who is Elvis as far as the Church of England is concerned) deliver the sermon in our church. There was something that appealed to me about having the opportunity to listen to a beautifully educated, highly intelligent man—wearing an extremely silly hat.

I was not disappointed. He was brilliant and said one thing in particular that stuck in my memory. "People with no sense of humor have no sense of proportion and shouldn't be put in charge of anything," he said.

I had no idea the old archbish knew anything about how golf's major ruling bodies run the game, did you? Thank heaven we don't have to listen to weekly sermons from them.

In closing, dearly beloved, let me say this: I am lucky enough to have friends of all denominations, all of whom are aware that I won't take them, or myself, too seriously.

I'll wear a yarmulke, sit in the lotus position (although I'll need help to get out of it), get on my elbows and knees, and say the Lord's Prayer—just to cover all the bases. But, as far as I'm concerned, it's all just after-life insurance. And that's coming from a man who works outside with an aerial on his head. I'm still pretty quick to get inside when the sky turns purple.

The wife wants to play golf. How can I dodge this bullet?

— *Preston Schroer, Brewster, Minnesota*

You have several options:

1. Homicide

2. Suicide

3. Self-mutilation

4. Send her to McCord/Kostis golf school.

5. Make her watch "The Big Break."

6. Divorce her.

7. Invite your regular foursome over for an intervention.

8. Constantly wager with her for sexual payoffs and beat the pants off her, sort of.

9. Insist on attending her all-girls bridge club afternoon.

Good luck.

That Dog Will Hunt

'Tis the season to toss the sticks under the stairs, whip out the trusty shotgun and head for quail country. Since 1993, when I moved to Texas and became a bonafide redneck Southern-gentleman trainee with several shotguns I couldn't hit a flying rhino with, my life has improved dramatically.

In a Neanderthal way, hunting is similar to golf. Since the dawn of time, sweaty Homo sapiens have been roaming the countryside sending badly aimed missiles at targets, cursing loudly and avoiding hazards. Mammoth have tusk—Ugga make spear. Ugga find ball—swing club. Bird fly—Browning make Citori shotgun. It's simple evolution, and as far as I'm concerned anyone who's willing to kill a mosquito or a cockroach shouldn't have a moral problem with some guy who's willing to sit up a tree in the dead of winter, making deer sneezes and moose farts so he can take one shot at a sofa with horns. Still, big-game hunting is not my cup of tea. I'm too squeamish to kill anything furry, and the size of what I shoot at is determined largely by a pathetic instinct for survival: I refuse to kill anything that, should it fall and land on my head, is big enough to kill me back. So I reckon my size limits out at a pheasant.

Where was I?

Oh yes, golf. The most obvious similarity between golf and wing shooting is between the caddies and the dogs. Dogs are just like caddies, except they smell better and are easier to train. They have better manners, too. A bird dog will give you the correct line and a fair idea of the distance, and if you miss, it will hardly ever say, "Hey, it's not my fault, porkwad." And a dog always knows where its balls are.

Still, the whole concept of bird hunting with dogs was confusing to me at first. I'd heard the story of the Irishman who tried it but gave up because he couldn't throw his retriever high enough. But on my first quail hunt, down in the cowboy country of south Texas, my buddies T.D. and Buck soon straightened me out.

There I was, decked out in full regalia, with my fancy kit and a brand-new gun—like a 28-handicapper with alligator spikes and a staff bag full of shiny Hogan blades—when a swarm of birds came bursting up from under my boots and nearly made me soil my chaps. As the fluffy little buggers whizzed off in 17 directions, I sprang into action, pausing only to make sure that my left shoulder was in front of my left foot, my stance was about shoulder width, and my ball position safely clear of any waist-high cactus. By this time the nearest bird was safely over the Mexican border, but, hell, I took a shot anyway, and during the course of the next few hours, I took a lot more. I'm not sure that I ever missed in front of a single bird. It was like hitting everything fat! The following day I continued this fine form, prompting T.D. and Buck to say that if I shot any farther behind I might at least get lucky and kill one from yesterday.

The next covey was of blues, and one was kind enough to balk in midair at the sound of T.D.'s gun, change direction and, for a moment, hang himself up like a feathery dinner-gong about 60 feet in front of me. There was no lead—or talent—required to hit my first quail, so I shouldered my Beretta and let fly.

"Clink," went the firing pin.

"What?" went T.D., and "S---!" went I. For the love of Ted Nugent in a tutu, what were the odds that my first misfire would come at that very moment? There's no way of calculating, but I will tell you this: They got a lot better when I factored in the ChapStick I'd loaded in the top chamber. As I explained to T.D., I wasn't trying to kill the blue—just moisturize it.

Imagine if it were illegal to play golf for two-thirds of the year. A bummer, yes, but how great you would feel on opening day! That's how I feel about wing shooting. Hey, I'm still crappy, but I'm in love with the whole scene—the birds, the guns, the clothes, the countryside, the comradeship, the discipline, and especially the dogs. How I love the hounds! After the hunt I like to spend a little quality time patting and stroking, gently removing grass burrs and cactus spines from every soft fold and crevice with a pair of rubber-tipped tweezers, applying soothing ointment—and then doing the same for the dogs.

Recently, I reached into my basket—by the john, of course—and found a *Golf* magazine issue. I read your "That Dog Will Hunt" SideSpin story and almost broke the john laughing when I read the part about the ChapStick in the chamber.

The reason I laughed so hard was that about 50 years ago (yes, 50!) a friend of mine (Butch Jaworski) and I were hunting rabbits (or whatever popped up). Butch had a single shot 410 and had a head cold, and I had a JC Higgins bolt action 16 ga. (Nothing but the best!)

Well, a pheasant popped up. Butch took a shot, and of course, he missed. He quickly reached into his pocket for another shell and reloaded and all we heard was a "click." We both looked down at his 410, which was pointed downward, and out of the end of the barrel came sliding out his ChapStick. I told him that, at least now, the pheasant could breathe okay and then ran like hell.

This is a true story. But what the hell, we had fun anyways. In fact we have (or at least I have) more fun retelling this story than we had when we were hunting.

Keep up those Sidespin stories. I love 'em!

—— *Bill Balyszak, Auburn, New York*

Lovely story Billy. But why did you run? Were you afraid he was going to moisturize you?

A Slippery Slope Away
From the Course

Hey, this is great! I'm in Snowmass, Colorado, with my wife and kids, and I don't even know who won at Doral! For the first time in my life, I'm going skiing, and for the first time in 25 years I'm trying to learn a new athletic pastime. Having reached a high level of proficiency at my only other chosen sport, the feeling of being a complete beginner is a strange one indeed.

I felt like the original duck out of water, or a 24-handicapper on the practice tee at the Masters, when I first snapped on my skis and tried to shuffle forward. My wife, Anita, pointed out, I should probably wait until I got outside into the snow. She is a really good skier, and she booked me private lessons with a fantastic coach, Grisha, the mountain guide from Chamonix in the French Alps. For the first day, I was a one-man avalanche, as witnessed by Tom and Melissa Lehman, amongst others. I bumped into them at the top of one of the lifts by chance, and they had a good chortle at me as I cartwheeled down Fanny Hill, one of Snowmass's green slopes.

The reason I'm telling you this is because I've found so many similarities between skiing and golf. (This ought to be good.) Firstly, if you are going to learn quickly, you have to start with a good instructor. I've been lucky to find a great one, and like all great teachers, Grisha is able to transfer to me not only his knowledge but the way that he feels, as he glides effortlessly down the slopes. Never mind the importance of balance, or the transfer of weight, or alignment of skis, or any of the physical skills that are required. Like a child learning to walk, I have learned by falling down, and getting up again. Grisha has kept me in the present, not worrying about what might happen, but rather focusing deeper and deeper on what *is* happening. I've learned that, just like in golf, where if you are afraid you might miss from four feet, you probably will, in skiing if you are afraid to fall, you've probably fallen already. More to the point, you won't remember why.

After three days with Grisha, I'm really skiing, and able to go up and down with my wife and sons. My boys are living proof that the theory above works. The only thing they're afraid of is that the lifts might close. Yesterday, I skied/fell down my first blue slope, and I don't care if they have to use a crane to get me into the 15th tower at Augusta, I'll be there. I remember my early days of learning golf, swinging on my own on the range, maybe four large buckets of frustrating tops, duffs, and shanks. Then my first real lesson with someone who knew how to let me feel it. One came right out of the middle of the clubface. It felt sweet and effortless, and I was mesmerized watching it fly. That's a feeling I do remember. It was the bug biting me.

My buds and I just finished playing 70 holes of golf in one day. We played the TPC at Deer Run. I was wondering, what is the most golf you have ever played in a day?

— *Jeff Panozzo*

You idiot, you have no life. Who in their right mind would play 70 holes in a day when they could spend the time eating, drinking, sleeping, and breaking wind?

I haven't played more than nine since 1996.

The Mighty Hunter

For all of us on the CBS golf crew, the time between when we quit for the season and start up again the following year is precious. Anyone who travels for a living knows that the size of the pile of crap on his or her desk is directly proportionate to the amount of time spent away, and in this road wiener's case, that means it's usually December before there is any time for fun and games.

During the midseason break, I didn't exactly master fly fishing, despite days of standing waist-deep in 40-degree water, so this winter, under the tutelage of a certain L. Wadkins, I decided to take a crack at becoming an expert quail hunter. Two geniuses with guns, against a bunch of feathery little farts that have a tendency to fly in a herd—I'd seen it on ESPN Outdoors, and no one ever misses the damn things, so I figured it wouldn't take me long to get the hang of it.

Wadkins had assured me that there were a lot of similarities between wing shooting and golf. Because I know nothing about guns, I dispatched She-Who-Must-Be-Obeyed to purchase the necessary firearms. (I would have gone with Wadkins, but given his legendary ability to piss people off, I thought it better not to go any place where I might get caught in crossfire.)

My wife is one of those Southern girls who can bake a cake in the morning, shoot the balls off a squirrel from 50 yards (with an iron sight) in the afternoon, then fit into a very, very little black dress at night. She came back with a sweet little Beretta over/under 28 gauge, and a big, black, nasty-looking Benelli 12, capable of holding five 3 $1/2$ inch shells.

I'm no expert, but even I know the 28 is a quail gun, while the Benelli is a weapon of mass destruction. Knowing full well it was a stupid question, I asked her what it was for. "It's for when you get tired of missing quail in South Texas, and you want to miss a pheasant in South Dakota," she said.

"Har-de-har, har," I said, and snatched the Benelli from her. I looked knowledgeably into the empty chamber, pushed the button to close the action, nearly cut the tip off my right thumb, and despite a magnificent effort, never even got close to looking like it didn't hurt. Shaking her head, she walked off to find my life insurance policy.

A few days later, after two stitches and several sporting clay lessons from Jeanie Almond at the Elm Fork Shooting Park in Dallas, I discovered there are indeed similarities between golf and shooting. Like, when your coach is standing behind you, showing you where your weight and your head should be, it will become easier and you'll wonder why you were so bad. Then when she's not, it'll come back to you.

When it was time to head for Hebbronville, Texas, I had improved enough to be crap with both guns, but as forecasted, particularly crap with the 28. However, as I was to shoot with real shooters, I reluctantly left the blunderbuss in the safe, slipped the Beretta into a soft case, packed my field-fronted camo, headed for Love Field, and boarded a King Air with Buck and

Luke. Wadkins was coming down the next day with T.D. and Jim. I'd been looking forward to this for months, but suddenly I realized that I was actually going hunting! I felt like Davy Crockett. Then it struck me. I was heading into the original cowboy country with Lanny, T.D, Jim, Buck, and Luke, and my name was "Dave." It sounded like five hunters and a hair stylist—not a good start.

From the start it was fairly obvious this was going to be a first-class affair. The Eschelman-Vogt Ranch covers 100,000 acres of south Texas, about 50 miles from Laredo. Will Vogt met us in a Suburban and took us to the ranch house, where Buck immediately locked the keys in the car, along with all the guns, and worse still, his Preparation H. It was a disaster, and if you don't believe me, try walking for miles after small birds through waist-high brush and cactus, with no gun and a sore ass.

Luckily enough, "Fingers" Feherty was on the scene, and within a matter of an hour and 20 minutes, with a flat screwdriver, a towel, and a coat hanger, I had us back in. Back when I was keen on that stuff and they were making decent quality hangers, it would have taken 30 seconds, but thankfully GM is still GM.

Eager to get going the following morning, I settled in my room, popped an Ambien, and drifted off to sleep. Twenty minutes later I woke up to a cold, wet nose in the old crotcheroonie. Abby, one of the ranch's Labrador retrieving rovers, had fancied a nocturnal nuzzle, but sadly she quit long before I could get excited about it. Feeling cheated, I stared alternately at the ceiling and my watch. At 4 a.m. I gave up, turned on all the lights, and read from cover to cover *The Call of the Quail*, a book of quail hunting articles by different authors. Typical—and just like golf—a dozen different theories.

In the morning, I knew even less about quail hunting. A blanket of fog hung over the property, and Will said the other boys wouldn't get into Hebbronville International Airport, Yacht Club, and Art Gallery unless their Citation V had curb feelers. "Oh, dear, what a pity. Never mind, let's hunt," said the rest of us.

We climbed into a special truck and sat on seats over the dog boxes, each of which held some kind of pointing pooch. Abby's somewhat arthritic looking husband, Dudley, sat at our feet, and after a short drive into the property along a sand road, Robe, the guide, hit the brakes, leapt out, and released the hounds. Talk about cool. Two of my favorite things in life are dogs and caddies, and apparently, quail dogs are both, although I must admit I've never had a caddie who writhed around on his back and wanted his tummy tickled.

Dudley, who moments earlier had looked like he might need a canine wheelchair, suddenly turned into Studley of the turbocharged nostrils. The German shorthairs, Tipper and Oiseau, shot out of the gates and immediately began crisscrossing in front of the truck, working their way to the tune of Robe's yelps and whistles. Within seconds, Tipper went as rigid as a tuning fork, and as if by magic, Oiseau spun around so fast I swear I heard her tail crack like a whip.

She leopard-crawled into a similar point about five yards from her partner, two corners of the triangle. I looked at the point where the lines through their bodies intersected, and saw the covey hunkered down. The dogs had given the exact line and yardage, and I had the right club and no ability. My heart was pounding as Robe released them with a grunt, and with a flurry of wing beats the birds shot up and out. Three pops, and a bird each for Luke and Buck. For me, the sudden realization that the safety has to be off. I was right on the fluffy little creature, too.

Over the next two hours, we saw, and shot at, ten coveys, and I realized that for the first time in my life, I was the "am" in the pro-am. I was the guy with the brand-new Hogans and the $900 snakeskin shoes who couldn't hit the sea off the deck of the *Nimitz*.

The great thing about having me along, though, was that with a 15-bird bag limit, the other two got in more shootin', which cheered them immensely. Yee-freakin'-haw! Four hours later the fog had burned off, and Wadkins, T.D, and Jim arrived, looking bloodthirsty. That afternoon, I accompanied our lead analyst on the hunt, which was like a biathlon, or as Robin Williams puts it, "a Norwegian drive-by."

That boy can put some lead in the air, and a lot of it goes in the right direction, too. Type A+ wouldn't describe him. After a rare miss, I thought the little ratbag was going to fly after the damn birds himself. But like the frustrated hacker who gives up on the 17th and then suddenly hits a couple of beauties, I got a few toward the end, so as we piled into the King Air to head for Luke's hunting camp at Cotulla, I figured I'd be better the next day.

At Cotulla International Speedway and Polo Club, we were greeted by two of the greatest characters I've ever met: Higton Compton and Taggart Mills. Higgy is 6-foot-5 and slim enough to look like the T in Texas with his bigger John B's on his head, and together with his runnin' buddy Taggart, they looked like Clint Eastwood and his demented Scottish cousin. They loaded our gear into a couple of Luke's trucks, and we headed through the vast, sprawling metropolis of Cotulla, and then into the inky black darkness down another dirt track.

After listening to Higgy's gleeful snake stories from the previous day, I decided I'd be wearing my boots to bed, and sleeping on top of Wadkins. As it turned out, it was the bottom bunk for me. T.D. got the single and Lanny slept up top, but seeing him trying to get up there was worth the price of a ticket. What an athlete. I haven't laughed that hard since the Browns beat the Ravens, and the dismount in the morning was even funnier. It was like watching a garden gnome fall off a picket fence.

Before we started that morning, I learned a few things, like how to put my snake chaps on the right way, and that you have to wear jeans or something underneath. Pitiful, but after seeing Wadkins naked on the toilet, I had a mental picture of the Village People, so it was an honest mistake.

By this time I'd had a chance to get a good look at the equipment the other boys had, and I'd decided mine was much prettier. My gun was angle ported, had extended choke tubes, and there was hardly a nick on the stock. Luke, who for some reason was duct-taping the top of his boots to his field-fronted jeans, was shooting with a battered 20 gauge.

I thought I was hunting with Martha Stewart, but as it turned out, the duct-tape idea was brilliant. I spent half the morning trying to dig what can only be described as spherical pins and hypodermic needles out of my shins.

We hunted that morning from an orange-and-black zebra-painted truck the boys had named "The Disco Donkey." Its side panels were scored with "South Texas pinstripes" left by the thorns.

Everything that grows in South Texas has either a thorn or a blade, and this land is quail land and nothing else. One head of cattle per 80 acres is all it will support. When we landed, I thought how ugly and featureless the landscape was. But as we sat up top for a breather and a late Budweiser breakfast sprinkled with lime tequila salt, Lanny spotted a fast-moving fog bank rolling across the tops of the Mesquite, and within minutes the visibility was down to a couple of hundred feet. It was eerily still and quiet, but for a sweet whistle from a nearby quail.

Suddenly, it seemed to me that it was beautiful, and we could be on St. Andrews or Royal County Down. It was time to go home, and as we got down to let the dogs back in the boxes, I spotted the bird that had been whistling. Luke had stayed on the Disco Donkey, but Lanny and I were loaded and dangerous.

It was a blue, sometimes called a scaly quail, and it was the first I'd ever seen. Even from 50 or 60 feet I could see the snake-like pattern on its breast. As the little prehistoric link between reptile and bird hunkered down to fly, I turned to Lanny and said, "Let it go, it's been a great trip."

He looked at me, shouldered his lovely Beretta and nodded his head wistfully. With a buzz of wings, the bird jumped up and sailed toward cover. "Yup, it sure has, partner," Lanny said, smiling.

I turned to head back to the truck, and there was one loud bang, followed by a chuckle. He'd vaporized it with the first barrel. It's probably why he won a PGA and I didn't.

I love your online golf instruction section on the website. Good stuff and funny. So I have to ask... When are you going to do a golf instruction book, or maybe a video? Golf the Feherty way.

— *Vern Suesse, Phoenix, Arizona*

HEY, VERN... Did you write that *Cat in the Hat* thing? My kids love that stuff. Green eggs and ham and all that. Brilliant. I've just finished a book on the history of the Ryder Cup and I'm not writing any more for a while, especially not on golf. I hate golf. I've used up my store of words and I have to let my head refill before I can go back for more.

A Tip of the "Cider Cup"

I haven't ventured outside of the good old U.S. of A. for a while now, so like many of you dear readers, I'm a little unfamiliar with some of the new faces on the European Tour. In fact, if Henrik Stenson bit me on the ankle I wouldn't know for whom I should be limping.

So, in the name of research into drinks with one ice cube, and despite the threat of mad cows with hooves in their mouths, I have decided to mount an expedition to Ireland and England the week before and the week of the Ryder Cup.

I am brushing up my native accent in a vain attempt to talk the way I did before I became a Texan while headed for the great used-to-be-known. As any great explorer will tell you, the keys to a successful expedition are preparation and personnel, so I am plotting everything in advance and assembling a posse of highly trained hangers-on.

I'm coming home on a boys' trip, and, as usual, I'm taking my wife for protection. But this time I'm also bringing a bunch of idiot Americans with me! People at home will be so impressed, I'm telling you.

It seems that everybody has his own Ryder Cup-style tournament these days. It's the golfing equivalent of a tailgate party, but I'm determined to make this one unlike any other. Like Hatfield versus McCoy, it's bound to end in tears, so this year I thought I'd simulate the disaster with a few of my own family and friends the week before the real Cup.

Normally, I try to get back to Ireland at least once a year to visit the old kinfolk, but a splinter group of these idiots have discovered where I live, and recently they've been camping out in front of my Sub-Zero on an all-too-regular basis. That sort of takes away my main reason for going home, because when I do, there's usually a bunch of them waiting for me there as well.

Not that I want to give the impression there is anything wrong with my relatives. No, no, absolutely not. It's just that they all appear to be insane, that's all. In fact, I feel that there is considerable evidence to suggest that I may be from an entirely different species, or planet, or something. But before you go assuming I am the black sheep of the family and therefore hold some kind of grudge against the rest of them, consider this: I have a second cousin who actually is a black sheep. His name is Digby, and he's already seeing someone.

Every team needs a doctor, so I am taking my brain surgeon, Dr. Mark Cwikla, who is a two-handicap and is capable of drinking like a halibut when pressed. Then, of course, we have to think about transport, so I'm bringing along Bobby Rodriguez, a.k.a. "B-Rod," who runs the Porsche Store in Dallas. As far as I am concerned, everybody should have a tame Porsche dealer as a designated driver.

Bobby is very sober and very, very fast, which may be useful around the Belfry, as the roads will no doubt be infested with police, who have a tendency to drive very badly indeed.

Mike Abbott, the director of golf at the Vaqueros Club just

outside Dallas, is being commissioned as the American team captain for no other reason than the fact that he is fatter than me and he is American. Bruce Turbow is a friend of mine who now lives in Austin and is coming along because he is a rich idiot who appears to do absolutely nothing but smile. I want to know how he does it.

On the other side of the ditch, there will be a welcoming committee for me and my merry band of Yanks. Howard Baws—who has been previously reported in these pages as the owner of the most photogenic genitals in the history of golf, and a man who hits his wedge two hundred yards (and every other club progressively shorter) —will be present, but probably not correct.

Chris Mitchell, the man who had the great misfortune to look after my business affairs for 14 years, will be there, along with Ian Carlin, who is my brother-in-law and a recovering alcoholic, largely because he is married to my sister. Finally, my father, a man who has absolutely no intention of recovering from anything, is coming along to act as team philosopher. In fact, most people, after coming into contact with my father, have to recover from him. He will be the captain of the European "Cider Cup" team.

I'm calling it the Cider Cup, after the very strong alcoholic apple drink from the west country of England, where the event will be played. Every pub has its own version of it called "scrumpy," which is also a pretty good way to describe how most people feel after a couple of pints. It's like apple-flavored lighter fluid.

The venue for this historic hysteria will be the Trevose Golf Club down in the county of Cornwall, where the members are among the most hospitable in the world. Also, most of them have a screw loose somewhere, which makes them the ideal hosts for an event such as this, in which the only rules will be: "Smoke yer own, find yer own, and keep up."

I am the one and only referee, and I will be doubling as the scrumpy cart girl. (Don't worry, by the time they've played nine I will be the most attractive thing they ever laid eyes upon.) The referee's decision will be final, and arguing, although not mandatory, will certainly be encouraged.

There are only two four-balls involved, which makes the Cider Cup the perfect size for dinner. A table should never have more than an eight-idiot-to-one-referee ratio.

Also, the event will be 36 holes in one day—foursomes in the morning, a four- hour lunch, and an afternoon four-ball that in all likelihood will end up being nine holes, punctuated by some tremendous burping.

After the fracas at Brookline, the European Cider Cup team has a lot to prove. The American side is not a particularly strong one, but it has one thing going for it, which, on this side of the Atlantic at least, is always perceived to be an advantage: it's American.

There will be few similarities to the real Cup, I fear. For a start, there will be only a very small jeering crowd at the Cider Cup, and absolutely no official functions, so that the players can concentrate fully.

Also, on the first tee, to decide who plays together, all the players on both sides will throw their balls in the air at the same time. (This is something they should consider for the real event. I can see Lord Derby now, staring down his nose and saying, "All right, chaps, who owns the Flying Lady?")

The Cider Cup will be what the Ryder Cup was always meant to be: A bunch of people brought together by a pastime, divided by a contest, and ultimately united again by simply having taken part in a celebration of the last pure sport on earth.

The Ryder Cup is natural selection (plus two picks) in action, all for bragging rights and to hell with money. Underneath the hospitality of the hosts, and the gratitude of the guests, there will burn a fierce desire to win, just for the opportunity of being able to brag in fun, and to heighten the anticipation for the next meeting in two years' time.

If it weren't for the rhetoric on television and herds of sheep-like writers stampeding back and forth between the camps and bleating their he-said/she-said stories, the way the players really feel would shine through.

Having said that, I don't care if you've never heard of half the European side, we're still going to destroy the vile capitalist pigs of the evil American Golfing Empire. I was on the 1991 team at Kiawah, pal, and no one had heard of me, either.

Of course, we lost. But that's a minor detail. This time you're all doomed.

You are so young and still very talented. Why did you stop competing? I remember the '91 Ryder Cup matches. You were unstoppable.

— *Tobin Bogard, Newport Beach, California*

A perceptive person you are Tobin, but you left out fat, and yet strangely attractive. And I was un*bearable*, not unstoppable. Sam Torrance, Payne Stewart and an inordinate fear of letting my side down propelled me through the '91 Ryder Cup. That experience was as close as you can come to the electric chair without actually frying. Contrary to popular opinion, not all the Irish are thick. I knew I could never be number one at playing, but talking? Now that's a pig with a different snout.

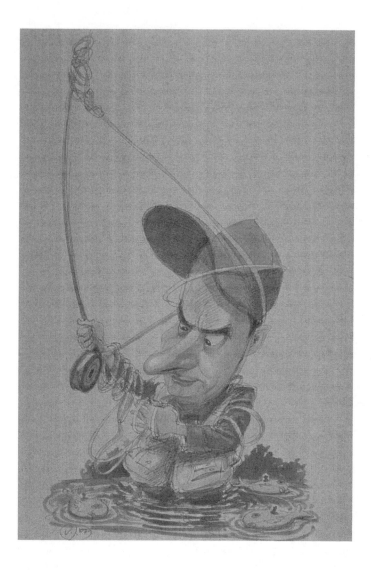

For the Birds

I have a confession to make. I didn't see a shot of the U.S. Open. Not one. Diddly-whatsit, zero, etc. I just flat out took U.S. Open week off, and went to Yellowstone with the breadsnatchers and She-Who-Must-Be-Obeyed, along with some of her family from Mississippi, and their whippersnappers. It was like the Griswold's Buick Roadmaster had crashed into the Beverly Hillbillies' truck, and they'd decided to make a week out of it. I decided to tackle up, get up to my waist in fast-flowing 40-degree water, and engage myself in an epic battle of wits with an invisible herd of chortling trout.

Oh yeah, I'm a fly fisherman now, and one of the best that was ever up a creek. After an hour, my scrotum had shrunk to the size of a California raisin, I couldn't feel my knees, but on the bright side, I was a little wiser than before. I didn't know that trout had a sense of humor. The bastards are sarcastic too, and at least as clever as me, which makes them damned smart, the scaly little creatures.

Okay, so I was crap at it. It doesn't make me a bad person, and in fact, from what I read about the U.S. Open, there are probably some parallels between what I did last week and what went on at Bethpage. I had about as much chance of catching one of those slippery little buggers as anyone had of catching Tiger. Also, there was a certain mystical pointlessness to my endeavor, which made it rather rewarding overall.

Actually, I got to the stage where it didn't matter whether or not I caught a fish, it was just fun to be there. I particularly enjoyed the crowd reaction to my efforts. There is nothing like having a few uncontrollable children around when you're trying to concentrate on something difficult, like fly-fishing.

Picture this: After several minutes of myopic fumbling, three loud yells, and one barely concealed hissy fit, you've managed to tie a fluffy hook the size of an anorexic gnat to an almost invisible piece of monofilament, when a four-year-old wearing a set of lavender foam antlers runs through the line, driving the hook deep into your index finger. Then she gives you a piece of half-chewed emu jerky, which you have to try, Daddy!

It's okay, all you have to do is drink a half-pint of Jack Daniels, push it through, nip off the barb, and pull it out. No biggie, but a rookie mistake. Up there, they like you to fish with barbless hooks anyway, so you might as well crimp 'em before you tie 'em.

I figured that one out just in time to drive a much larger imitation stonefly nymph into the back of my skull at about 120 mph. It's surprisingly loud when you take one that close to your ear, but it was a dawdle to get out compared to the wee caddis fly thingy. Lovely stuff.

There was a heckler in the crowd. It was a smartass osprey chick in a cluster of sticks at the top of a telegraph pole, and I could've sworn it was counting my attempts to present the fly in the right spot. It was taking me quite a while though, and it got bored. As I crocheted myself a pair of pale green underpants between the reel and the first guide hole on the rod, I spotted one of the parents, which had been perched in a nearby Douglas fir for some time.

Suddenly it dropped, as silent as snow from the branch, and fell into a low, smooth, impossibly fast glide. Surely to God it wouldn't, I was thinking to myself, but I felt the goosebumps rise on my forearms, as it leveled out inches above the water about a hundred feet in front of me. It barely broke the surface tension of the Madison river as it plucked a wriggling six-inch long silver blade from the water and without a wing beat, peeled hard left and up toward the nest. A yard above with full flaps, it touched down like a snowflake, beaked the fish toward the squealing infant, and slowly turned its head to look directly into my eyes.

That's how you do it, you moron.

Oh, yeah. I had that expression—you know, mouth the size and shape of a Cheerio, and eyebrows vanished into the hairline. Damn, I thought, what a show.

And this place is open to the public?

My father is a big golf fan and loves to play the game. We used to play every weekend until he was diagnosed with cancer and had to go through treatment. Could you please send him something to cheer him up? Thank you very much.

— *Andy, Atlanta, Georgia*

Certainly I will. I'll send him something I know will cheer him up. *You*. *You* are the reason he played every weekend with you. Your dad knows the value of time now, and every minute he spends with you will be precious, whether it's on or off the golf course. Make him promise to play again as soon as he can, and hold the old fart to it. Write to me and let me know when you play your next round, and I'll join you if I can. Good luck.

By the way, I once sent McCord a fart in a ziplock bag. If your father would like one, it would be my pleasure.

Human Stains

Once a year, She-Who-Must-Be-Obeyed forces me to go on a family holiday. I put up a manly resistance, feigning injury and sobbing, but it never works. The best I can negotiate is a compromise in which I attempt to fly-fish while the annoying fruit of my loins scare away the fish. I can't stand the beach so we go up a mountain, which makes me only slightly less grumpy. I'm a bad parent, in worse shape. Any higher than 3,000 feet and I get winded eating chips and salsa.

My ideal vacation is a week in front of my own refrigerator, bleary and unshaven, wondering what I don't need to eat next. At least it's home. I travel so much for work that I recognize the stains on the carpet at the Holidome in Flint and the Hilton Akron. And what really wads my Jockeys, particularly toward the end of the golf season, is using hotel bathrooms.

Okay, I might have a little problem in this area, but not without cause. For my 45th birthday, clearly haunted by the ghosts of skid marks past, She-Who-Must consigned all my white underpants to a well-ventilated fire and repurchased the same in black. Her move was vindicated by a steady burn punctuated by an occasional violent flare. And what's more, she says black makes me look smaller, which is good. I think.

On the road, my mood is black. No matter how crisp the linens or high the thread count, I still find it hard to get past the fact that I'm lying in the sweaty depression made last night by a 350-pound hamster farmer from Reno. Here's a little travel advice: The second-worst mistake any hostelry dweller can make is to open the door for room service wearing a hair net, surgical mask, rubber gloves, an adult diaper and black calf-length socks. The worst (because it leads to the second-worst) is to hold the bed linen up to the light. Fling open your drapes some morning and let the sun illuminate every silvery stain, translucent drool, and delicate dribble—testaments to the hotel's valiant struggle to conserve the earth's resources. A towel on the rack means you'll use it again—after the housekeeper wipes down your tub with it.

In Colorado I had a room with one of those sliding-door-over-the-tub, 16-nozzle showers. Nothing was labeled hot or cold, up or down. I aimed all the nozzles away from anything dangly and let it rip, hoping that if anything went wrong, my shrieks could be heard over the deluge. Of course, when I finally got the pressure and temperature regulated, the overhead nozzle wouldn't work. I had one foot in the soap dish and the other on the toilet when She-Who-Must came in to investigate, and the subsequent photograph hasn't been easy to explain.

The aforementioned birthday was celebrated with a total lack of mail, presents, or good wishes from the players of the PGA Tour, many of whom seem to be similarly ancient. I am going to respond by making stuff up about them. How about Jay Haas and Fred Funk, combined age 143, making the Presidents Cup team? As if the Presidents Cup matters. I thought it was an undergarment worn by Bill Clinton to protect the First Willy.

My offspring are forbidden to play golf for fear they might

like it and start asking me stupid questions. I get enough of that on television from our tower announcers. But on our family vacation I let down my guard and we went to play Putt-Putt. It was depressing and slow, but the worst part was that no one knew who the hell I was.

Rory, my youngest boy, made his first hole-in-one and proceeded to duck-walk around the windmill, playing air guitar, screaming, "I'm number one!" He told everyone his dad was one of the greatest golfers ever, it was hereditary, blah blah.... So the man behind me, a hairy tank-top type with countless cross-eyed children, asked me how many holes-in-one I'd had.

"Eight," I answered truthfully, at which he and his ghastly brats began to snort and hoot.

"Shee-it, man," he said, slapping his hand on a fiberglass rock. "I've had 43!"

I told him I quit early to go into TV.

Have you ever taught She-Who-Must-Be-Obeyed how to play golf? Do you play (golf, that is) together? Your thoughts on the subject in general.

— Vladimir

Vlad. Have you lost your mind? No man should teach his wife to play, you cretin, and the reason is obvious. She might like it! Obviously, you're Russian, and it is questions like this that point out some of the disadvantages of freedom of the press. If the KGB were still a force, you would be clapped in irons and have electrodes attached to your testicles running to a car battery that would be switched on periodically until you promised to never bring up the subject again.

Shooting for Birdies... Off the Course

I went bird hunting last week in the Texas hill country with my wife, and I was struck once again, just as I was when I went skiing for the first time last year, by the similarities between golf and everything else in the universe.

I experienced the tension that all novices feel when they find themselves thrust into the company of experts, such as my wife, who could shoot the balls off a running ferret at a hundred yards, and Butch, our guide and instructor for the hunt. I was armed with my new 20-gauge gas-powered Beretta 3-shot special as we set off into the long grass in search of lunch. I must admit, I felt an almost primeval sense of power at the thought of actually eating what I was going to kill.

After two hours of loud banging and cursing, it became apparent that I was going to enjoy a lunch consisting of one empty Dr. Pepper can and the hindquarters of an English pointer called Rodney. The birdlife of the area was so safe from my advances that at one stage a hen pheasant actually tried to build a nest on the end of my barrel. It was embarrassing, and I was starting to think I had more chance of killing a bird by throwing one of the dogs in the air when an elderly chukar died of natural causes in midair right in front of me, getting me off the schneid.

Then Butch gave me a lesson. Wouldn't you know it, but my weight distribution was all wrong, my stance was constipated, and—knock me down with a feather—but I wasn't following through either! All of these are things that have been wrong with my golf game from time to time!

Just like a golfer that has been set straight, I shot much better that afternoon, killing a dozen or so birds, and almost bringing down a Southwest Airlines jet.

Just like a golfer, the following morning I couldn't have hit a flying heifer with a blunderbuss.

On a completely unrelated note, I have to admit I'm feeling a little nervous about this Thursday night's "Late Night Show," at the Phoenix Open, as I have just shot my first ever nude scene. The problem is, I was in the shower with Peter Kostis. No big deal you might say, these are the zeros. (I don't know, but somehow that doesn't sound as good as the nineties.)

Now, I'm pretty secure in my masculinity, but after doing this scene, I was seized by an urge to fluff up the pillows in my room and change all the window treatments. I was able to quickly exorcise the demons though, by lighting a fire on the carpet and painting a few bison on the walls. I'm fine now... honestly.

My cousin Douglas Rea grew up playing golf in Bangor, Northern Ireland. Any chance you knew him? He's about five years your senior.

— Brian Keith

I do know Dougie Rea and next time you see him tell him I'm still waiting for the money he owes me for taking his astonishingly homely sister to the dance at the Convent of the Mothers of Perpetual Pain. Better yet, I'm going to be in Bangor this month for an AT&T gig. Send me his address. I'll send a couple of my buddies from the RUC around to collect. By the way, he was a hell of a rugby player.

Eire She Blows

Fourteen years ago, right here on the Old Course, I hit the greatest shot of my career—a horrifyingly hung-over lilac long iron that won the Dunhill Cup for Ireland. Now my pal Sam Torrance and his son Daniel were leading the Dunhill Links pro-am, so I was on a mission to get behind the 18th green to surprise them. My first obstacle was a wee Jimmy in a flat hat, who was savagely guarding the media-and-players-only crossing point at the Road Hole.

"Excuse me, sir, I'm David Feherty," I said. "And I need to get over there to meet my best friend, Sam Torrance. I don't have a pass, but I captained the Irish team that won here against the English in 1990."

"Certainly ye did.... F--- off!"

So I bought a ticket, ran up through the town and saw them win. Sam had played rubbish, but 15-year-old Daniel won him 50 grand. I gave Sam a slap on the back, which as we say is "only 18 inches from a kick in the hole."

Then to Ireland we went, the family and I, back to 93 Clifton Road, Bangor, County Down, and the real reason for the trip— a hug from my mummy, who knows I'm famous. As always, she had a pot of cream of sheepskin soup on the stove. I felt better until I got to Bangor Golf Club, where the members had been charged 20 for the privilege of listening to a speech by the idiot child who, 27 years ago, dropped out of high school and turned pro with a 5 handicap. They'd only just stopped laughing about that, so it wasn't so hard to get them started again. Due largely to their heroic consumption of Cork Gin, I survived.

The next stop was my old high school, Bangor Grammar, which has a history of academic excellence, and now a tradition of having truants back to speak at Speech Day. I said it was nice that a pupil didn't actually have to *finish* in the school to qualify for such an honor—a line that went down better with the boys than with the faculty. I told of how I used to sit in class, listening to the drone of lawn mowers outside, inhaling the smell of grass cuttings and Simon Mercer (who sat in front of me), dreaming of sweet swings with battered old clubs and Titleists with elastic hanging out. I told them I used to go to roll call, then sneak out to the club, where I'd spend all day in the pro shop, working with glue, solvents, and naked flame. What an education!

After my speech they gave me a diploma and, more important, a schoolboy's cap with a gold tassel, which I told them would increase the pleasure of my evening spanking immeasurably—a statement that, strangely enough, the faculty seemed to enjoy more than the boys.

Now the Fehertys set off for Donegal and a few days at the Fort Royal Hotel in Rathmullan, a favorite spot of mine. It rained for three days, prompting the postmaster to say, "It's keepin' the dust down nicely." On my parents' 50th anniversary (at press time there was no clear leader in their 50-year argument), I loaded Mum and Dad into a rental rocket along with She-Who-Must-Be-Obeyed and Erin-the-Terrifyingly-Beautiful-Small-

Person. My sister Debbie and her long-suffering husband, Ian, piled into another car with Murphy the black lab; Kiva the 125-pound boxer; DJ, a moronic Irish fox terrier; and Bart the cat. To a casual observer, it looked like the pound had just been robbed by two mental patients. On the way, I saw their car swerve violently and later found out it was caused by a surreptitious fart from my sister (since denied), which was hideous enough to make DJ the terrier hurl on her lap, which in turn made Bart the cat crap all over the backseat. When poor Ian rolled down a window, Kiva the heavyweight boxer jumped at the opportunity to either escape or commit suicide. I used to share a room with my sister, and I would have done the same.

We sped to Portnablagh, where the surf was pounding over the sea wall. I love that crap and pride myself on being able to read the waves. I trundled the car down the pier so we could feel the power of Poseidon. A swell burst over the concrete and produced a giggle or two, so I let my window down a bit. Four seconds later the alarm was blaring, the doors were locking and unlocking themselves, my mother's hair was plastered to her skull, and there was a little winkle in my underpants.

All in all, it was a normal outing for the Fehertys, down to the return of two rental cars, which we nicknamed "Shite" and "Briny." I'd taken the collision damage waiver on mine, and what with the collision damage being caused by a wave....

They argued, but I didn't waver.

Are you serious? You haven't played more than 9 holes in a day since '96. What's your excuse(s)? I'm glad my wife doesn't read your articles. She'd expect the same from me.

— Ritchie

I'm glad your wife doesn't read the stuff I write either. Hell, *my* wife doesn't read my articles. I get paid to talk and write about golf, not play it. McCord's the only idiot I know who still thinks he can play the game. You don't see Marv Albert shooting hoops or Phil Simms tossing the old pigskin around when he's not announcing football, do you? You think Howard Cosell used to spar with Muhammad Ali? I can still play but not like I used to when I had to in order to pay my bar tab. Besides, my balls hurt when I hit 'em now.

Dogballs

I t was one of those spur-of-the-moment ideas that usually turn out to be disastrous: A squirming cluster of beagle puppies in a wire cage by the roadside, tended by a nasty-looking hillbilly with a wooden pickup truck, four teeth and a shitty attitude. I paid $350 bucks for the littlest one, a pitiful grublike runt with a broken tail, no bigger than a hamster, weighing in at less than a pound. A few days later, after She-Who-Must-Be-Obeyed had stopped yelling at me, we found out from the vet that the feeble wee man was from a puppy mill in Oklahoma, chemically dependent, and incontinent. Hey, I'm not from Oklahoma, but already we had a couple of things in common! Somehow I knew I would love this dog like no other.

His tail had been slammed in a cage door, broken in two places, and clearly he had been left in that position for a long time, as his wagging tackle had set into a tiny "Z" at its tip. So we called him Ziggy, short for Zigmoid, but sadly his cute deformity had to be docked, as he would hang it up on things, making him squeal like a baby.

We'd never had a beagle before, and people were preparing us with tales of psychotic chewing and howling trauma, but our resident house-hound, Willard the Wonder Mutt, was positively dog-smacked about the new arrival. At first he thought it was great, something that he could hump around the den, or at least rough up a little, but once Ziggy got a little strength, the hard-headed little houndling began to beagle Willard. Okay, so I'm a relatively new beagler, but as far as I can tell, the word "beagle" can be either a noun or a verb. I think that beagling might be the most faithfully dog-like behavior in the canine world. A beagle's human is there only to provide too much food, followed by the kind of vigorous arse- and back-scratching that a beagle deserves, simply *because* he's a beagle. If Ziggy isn't immediately visible, then there's an odds-on chance he's buried in the most expensive throw-pillow in the house, and not before he's given it a horrible savaging. I can drop an M&M anywhere in my house and Ziggy will find it within 45 seconds, and I swear if I were daft enough to hide the rest of the packet in the house next door, he would spend the night tunneling through a hardwood floor and four feet of concrete slab to get at it, pausing only to kill several squirrels and bang the crap out of an apparently dead possum. Hey, if it's still warm....

I think I mentioned it before, but I love this dog. His life's mission is to be at the center of mine all of the time. He is under my feet, in my bed, on my lap in the car, down my throat if I just ate, and hammered right up the crack of my arse if I just farted. I used to be able to blame the occasional sly one on Willard, but now I have a tricolor scratch 'n' sniff lie detector that rats me out in an instant. If I had two of them, they might meet at my pancreas. The thing I admire most about the little prince is that, in his own mind, he is so *obviously* the highest form of intelligence on the planet, and yet he carries himself with the sweet humility and groveling gratitude that only a dog can possess. In any other creature such behavior would be revolting.

And Willard, the simple wiener-schnauzer-gerbil-hound who used to be top dog, has been transformed from the Wonder Mutt into the mutt that wonders. I dole out chew sticks, one apiece, and Ziggy calmly takes his and buries it either in a houseplant, underneath a sofa cushion, or in my suitcase, which lies half-packed most of the time on my dressing room floor. (To find a slimy piece of rawhide in your last clean pair of underpants is always a nice surprise in a hotel room.) Then he returns to the Willard the underdog to give him a serious beagling. No violence mind you, he just uses a relentless, blink-free *"I'm the beagle, asshole!"* stare that turns Willard into pussy-putty within seconds. With the efficiency of a turbo-charged wood-chipper, he eats Willard's treat, goes back to the houseplant, retrieves his own, and eats it too. Willard seems completely unperturbed, but then one of the reasons dogs are better than humans is because the losers among them are *happy* to follow.

My life is weird. I have a late flight here, a bad flight there, here a prop, there a jet, occasionally a bed wet, and *waaay* too many old McDonald's for dinner. It's hard to find anything consistent on the road, but I do know this. When I stumble in at one o'clock on a Monday morning from Memphis, or Detroit, or Milwaukee, or wherever, even if I'm still wearing golf shoes and plastered with old sunscreen and stale sweat, there will be a pair of wagging tails at the back door. Willard will try to lick me into a coma, and after Ziggy has rooted through my suitcase to make sure the smell of my laundry isn't from some forgotten, rotten pig's ear he, the 28 pounds of anointed hound, will allow me the privilege of scratching every square inch of him before he roots his way under the bedsheets and molds himself into the crook of She-Who-Must-Be-Obeyed's legs. Oh, how we adore this dog, but then again (as he constantly reminds us) we're only human.

Your bio says you live in Irving, Texas. This makes little sense, based on my own experience in Irving. I flew into to Dallas-Fort Worth Airport for a conference in Dallas, but, since I registered late, the only place to stay was the Days Inn in Irving, half a mile from Texas Stadium, the one with the hole in the top for God to watch his Cowboys. It had been a long trip, culminating in having a native Texan, still working on freeway driving, take us from the airport to the Inn. Tired, hungry and THIRSTY, I stumbled down to the diner. The first thing I asked the cute little Texas thing waiting tables was, "What's on tap?" To which she answered, "We don't serve beer. Irving is DRY." Ignoring the contradiction of having a football stadium in a dry town, what is an Irishman doing in a dry town like Irving? Or have they entered the late 20th century?

— *Mike McKeown*

I don't live in Irving; I live in Dallas. Dallas is wet, very wet. Since I am aware Irving is dry, I have never even stopped for a red light there. The Irving police have a permanent warrant out for my arrest. For my part, I've begun a class action lawsuit on behalf of the residents of Irving as well as anyone who has had to pass through it citing cruel and unusual punishment. I'll keep you posted; you may be entitled to some compensation.

Road Trip 2

I'd never been on an organized golf holiday until a few years ago, when I conceived the first Cider Cup, contested in England between idiot friends of mine from both sides of the Atlantic. After conception I ran from responsibility. Mitch, my great pal and ex-agent, took care of the arrangements, from travel to lodging to tee times, and it went smooth as Nantz's bottom. But for the second go-round I wanted the boys to see my native Northern Ireland, so heroically I took the organizing upon myself. It was just 20 or so morons drinking and golfing—how hard could it be?

You know those nauseating golf novels in which the mystic game serves as a bilious backdrop for one man's journey of self-discovery, leading to the hurlingly obvious reaffirmation of that which he already knew to be true? This is the short version. Yes, friends, by taking the reins I confirmed that the biggest moron I know is still me.

I booked 10 rooms at the five-star Culloden Hotel weeks in advance. No problem there—until a snotty staffer called a few days before the Cup to demand info, else I'd have to cough up for no-shows. I was in the market for a little flexibility—six of these pillocks were going to arrive on a G4 whenever they damn well pleased—so after getting the Heisman I politely lost my reason and told them to insert the rooms where the sun doesn't shine, which, in Ulster, gave them plenty of options. I called the friendly Royal Hotel in my hometown of Bangor, which is within blundering distance of Fealty's, the best pub in town. Brilliant!

Okay, so the lads weren't thrilled with the rooms, or that I'd showed up at the wrong airport to fetch them, but never mind the minor details. Golf beckoned, and we tore up a lovely wee course called the Ava at Clandeboye. Then we all got bulletproof at Fealty's, the lads stumbled back to the Royal, and I took a bracing walk home around the seafront to Mom and Dad's house, pausing to get up off the ground only twice. Things were going swimmingly.

The next morning, I arrived at the hotel with a 24-seat bus and a NEW HANGOVER JOKE (pickled tongue?). Searching for bodies in last night's wreckage, I came up four short. A broken steam pipe had turned several rooms into a Turkish bath, and the G4 swine had escaped to, horror of horrors, the Culloden!

So, the pleb-filled bus set off to Royal Portrush, but halfway there the driver, overcome by cigar smoke, Guinness farts and Bushmills belching, took a wrong turn and went to Ballymena. Somehow, this was my fault. Anyway, the G4s took a cab, no one broke 100 in 50-mph squalls and we fled back to the Royal, where I almost soiled myself when I realized *I hadn't paid the greens fees*! Feherty, thy name is dirt.

A cell phone and AmEx card doused that fire, but my operational hell got even warmer when the G4s were forced to move from the Culloden to the Belfast Hilton and my pal Hollywood Anderson finally arrived, finagling a room at (where else?) the Culloden. Hollywood was wearing a lavender cashmere sweater with matching lavender FootJoys, and a positively dangerous pair of slacks I thought were peppermint but he dubbed "sea foam." (Sea foam is a brown scum where I come from.) Liberace was hitting the links.

But I digress. We played Kirkiston Castle the next day— another 17-vehicle, three-hotels-in-different-towns daytime nightmare, rescued only by a ferry to the astonishing Lobster Pot restaurant in Strangford. By now the official tour guide was catching heavy flak. Tomorrow was the final day at the world's greatest golf course, Royal County Down, and the nicest name I'd been called all week was "dorkwad." I beseeched Allah, Jehovah, Buddha and Dr. Phil: Decent weather please, or maybe an invisibility cloak.

The next morning, at the only moment I took my bulging eyeballs off the road, the damn bus took another wrong turn. The drive to RCD is about 45 minutes—we took twice that. But while I was cursing Dr. Phil, it happened. As we rolled into Newcastle, County Down, the sun rent a hole in the clouds over the Mountains of Mourne and spread gold over the purple dome of Slieve Donard and on down the hill through the forest, over the town, and slowly began to light up the Irish Sea. Mouths hung open as we trundled into the parking lot. Then the wind died, and the day turned into a fairytale. Suddenly, the tour guide was a hero.

But I am never, *ever* doing it again.

As a 48-year-old golfer is it considered "girlie" to use hybrids, hacksticks, and fairway woods all the way up to a 7-iron? I carry no irons below the 7.

— *Jim Logemann, Phoenix, Arizona*

What the hell is a hackstick? There are a lot of things considered "girlie" in golf: pink tees, playing from the reds, culottes, Capri pants, NEVER giving a putt, arguing over rules you don't know, not watching your ball after you hit it, keeping score with the aid of a string of beads hanging from your bag, tassels on your shoes, little fuzzy balls that hang off the heels of your socks, Sesame Street character head covers, paisley bags and making little snowmen on the scorecard when you take an eight. But playing with the all-wood concept is fine. Kick some ass with your 11-wood pal. Most of us would be better players if we had enough balls to be a little more girlie.

Through the Looking Glass

I was looking through my old scrapbooks just yesterday, as my wife is in the process of updating them. It was quite a disturbing experience. My God, but I used to be thinner and better looking. Faded yellow newsprint images of a slender young Irishman, and stories of the high points of my career, mixed with the front page tabloid lows of my personal life, adorn the massive cardboard pages, each one like a slice of my life. As the newsprint becomes less faded, I gradually get larger, my face more corrupted by the travel and the aging and the stress, and all the things one does to combat them. I work in TV, but possess the perfect face for radio.

I've noticed I'm not alone, though, in my "Picture of Dorian Gray" decline. All of my colleagues from way back look a little different these days. I came across a youthful Darren Clarke between the pages, some 10 years or so into my career. He was then a chubby youth, but already in possession of the impish grin we saw so much of just a couple of weeks ago when he won the Andersen Consulting Match Play Championship. He and I are Ulstermen, and I have followed his career closely, from the time when I was actually capable of beating him. I am one of those white guys who looks like his ass has fainted, but the same could hardly be said of Darren. We used to tease him, telling him that with a backside like that he could kick-start a Jumbo Jet.

The inevitable Ryder Cup comparisons always come up when two such players go at it head-to-head as Darren and Tiger Woods did, and it's kind of a pity that we don't see more of it throughout the season. If we did, the U.S. golf viewing public would be treated to more great players like Darren, and the U.S. media would be less inclined to make the American Ryder Cup team such overwhelming favorites every two years. The players know the truth, just ask Hal Sutton or Tiger.

It's a funny thing, now that I have a camera pointed at me from time to time. I tend to spot all of my flaws. Just the other day, I received a bunch of photos of myself from CBS. You know, publicity shots that I sign and send to those poor souls that have such pitiful existences they feel the need to have me staring at them from the bathroom wall. The thing is, in this latest batch, I look halfway decent.

Of course, it turns out they were airbrushed.

Bye for now.

Love,
Dorian

Credits

WINTER

Fear of Flying—*Golf Magazine*, April 2003

Mailbag—My Typical Workweek, February 13, 2004

Rubberize My Room—Golfonline.com, February 21, 2001

Mailbag—Family Ties, September 16, 2004

Method to the Madness—*Golf Magazine*, June 2003

Mailbag—US vs. Them – And Pekkapickledpeppers, January 22, 2004

Everyone's an Expert—Golfonline.com, August 27, 2001

Mailbag—Fashion Police, March 12, 2004

Urinanalyst—Golfonline.com, May 16, 2001

Mailbag—Family Ties, September 16, 2004

Ad Addict—*Golf Magazine*, February 2004

Mailbag—My Thoughts on the '58 Masters Controversy, March 29, 2004

The Fine Art of Ganching—Golfonline.com, October 21, 1998

Mailbag—Wives, Commercials and Monty, December 1, 2004

The Stupidity Channel—*Golf Magazine*, May 2001

Mailbag—What's with the Goatee, March 1, 2004

Terminal Logic—Golfonline.com, May 17, 2000

Mailbag—Shinnecock Shenanigans, August 5, 2004

Don't Tell Me, You Have an Inner Ear Problem, Right?—Golfonline.com, January 24, 2001

Mailbag—Fashion Police, March 12, 2004

The Root of All Evil—*Golf Magazine*, June 1999

Mailbag—Fashion Police, March 12, 2004

A Goal and an Assist—Golfonline.com, April 23, 2002

Mailbag—What's With the Goatee, March 1, 2004

Dudley vs. Snidely—*Golf Magazine*, March 2002

SPRING

My Career High—*Golf Magazine*, January 2003

Mailbag—Birthday Wishes, September 2, 2004

What a Day That Was—Golfonline.com, September 20, 2000

Mailbag—My Thoughts on the '58 Masters Controversy, March 29, 2004

Practice Blows—*Golf Magazine*, December 2004

Mailbag—Baby, It's Cold Out There, December 15, 2004

Abducted by Aliens—Golfonline.com, July 28, 1999

Mailbag—Shinnecock Shenanigans, August 5, 2004

I Swooned at Troon—*Golf Magazine*, July 2004

Mailbag—Birthday Wishes, September 2, 2004

Right Club, Wrong Player—Golfonline.com, September 22, 1999

Mailbag—Me vs. McCord, June 4, 2004

Trophy Cases—*Golf Magazine*, August 2001

Mailbag—Family Ties, September 16, 2004

What's Old Is New Again—*Golf Magazine*, August 2003

Mailbag—Me vs. McCord, June 4, 2004

A Moving Experience—Golfonline.com, June 30, 1999

Mailbag—Fashion Police, March 12, 2004

Great Balls of Fire—*Golf Magazine*, August 1999

Mailbag—US vs. Them – And Pekkapickledpeppers, January 22, 2004

Captain Underpants and the Quest for Knowledge—Golfonline.com, September 6, 2000

Mailbag—My Typical Workweek, February 13, 2004

Knick and Knack—*Golf Magazine*, April 2001

Mailbag—Fashion Police, March 12, 2004

Information Overload—*Golf Magazine*, October 2002

SUMMER

Naked Came the Dangler—*Golf Magazine*, August 2004

Mailbag—The 2004 Masters, May 14, 2004

All Things Being Equal—*Golf Magazine*, May 2003

Mailbag—My Typical Workweek, February 13, 2004

In the Olympic Spirit—Golfonline.com, March 6, 2002

Mailbag—Why I Quit Playing, June 22, 2004

Rules of Engagement—*Golf Magazine*, March 2001

Mailbag—Why I Quit Playing, June 22, 2004

A Load of C.R.(A.A.)A.P.—*Golf Magazine*, November 2002

Mailbag—A Lesson on Charity, August 19, 2004

We're Not Worthy—Golfonline.com, July 26, 2000

Mailbag—A Lesson on Charity, August 19, 2004

I'm Marrying Tiger—*Golf Magazine*, March 2004

Mailbag—Wives, Commercials and Monty, December 1, 2004

Mailbag—US vs. Them – And Pekkapickledpeppers, January 22, 2004

The Thin Men—Golfonline.com, January 15, 2002

Mailbag—The 2004 Masters, May 14, 2004

The Life and Crimes of Heavy D—*Golf Magazine*, May 2004

Mailbag—What's With the Goatee, March 1, 2004

Aliens—Golfonline.com, August 21, 2001

Mailbag—Why I Quit Playing, June 22, 2004

Phil!—*Golf Magazine*, June 2004

Mailbag—The 2004 Masters, May 14, 2004

Smoke 'em If You've Got 'em—Golfonline.com, May 3, 2000

FALL

The Unholy One—*Golf Magazine*, August 1998

Mailbag—Wives, Commercials and Monty, December 1, 2004

That Dog Will Hunt—*Golf Magazine*, December 2003

Mailbag—Family Ties, September 16, 2004

A Slippery Slope Away from the Course—Golfonline.com, March 10, 1999

Mailbag—Birthday Wishes, September 2, 2004

The Mighty Hunter—*Golf Magazine*, April 2003

Mailbag—Me Vs. McCord, June 4, 2004

A Tip of the "Cider Cup"—*Golf Magazine*, September 2001

Mailbag—Why I Quit Playing, June 22, 2004

For the Birds—Golfonline.com, July 8, 2002

Mailbag—Why I Quit Playing, June 22, 2004

Human Stains—*Golf Magazine*, November 2003

Mailbag—Family Ties, September 16, 2004

Shooting for Birdies…Off the Course—Golfonline.com, January 26, 2000

Mailbag—Family Ties, September 16, 2004

Eire She Blows—*Golf Magazine*, January 2004

Mailbag—Wives, Commercials and Monty, December 1, 2004

Mailbag—*Texas Living*, November 17, 2004

Road Trip 2—*Golf Magazine*, February 2005

Mailbag—Nantz, McCord, Moe and Payne, October 27, 2004

Through the Looking Glass—Golfonline.com, March 8, 2000